THE PILGRIM'S COMPASS

THE PILGRIM'S COMPASS

Finding and Following the God We Seek

PAUL H. LANG

WESTMINSTER
JOHN KNOX PRESS
LOUISVILLE • KENTUCKY

First edition
Published by Westminster John Knox Press
Louisville, Kentucky

19 20 21 22 23 24 25 26 27 28—10 9 8 7 6 5 4 3 2 1

Unless otherwise indicated, Scripture quotations are from the New Revised Standard Version of the Bible, copyright © 1989 by the Division of Christian Education of the National Council of the Churches of Christ in the U.S.A., and are used by permission. Scripture quotations marked RSV are from the Revised Standard Version of the Bible, copyright © 1946, 1952, 1971, and 1973 by the Division of Christian Education of the National Council of the Churches of Christ in the U.S.A., and are used by permission.

Book design by Drew Stevens
Cover design by Eric Walljasper

Library of Congress Cataloging-in-Publication Data
Names: Lang, Paul H., author.
Title: The pilgrim's compass : finding and following the God we seek / Paul
   H. Lang.
Description: Louisville, KY : Westminster John Knox Press, 2019. |
   Identifiers: LCCN 2018044500 (print) | LCCN 2019002178 (ebook) | ISBN
   9781611649192 (ebk.) | ISBN 9780664264697 (pbk.)
Subjects: LCSH: Spiritual formation--Presbyterian Church.
Classification: LCC BV4511 (ebook) | LCC BV4511 .L36 2019 (print) | DDC
   248.4/851--dc23
LC record available at https://lccn.loc.gov/2018044500

CONTENTS

Acknowledgments   *vii*

1. Pilgrimage and the Emerging Church   1

2. Pilgrimage as the Home of Our Sojourning   18

3. Not All Who Wander Are Lost:
   Tools for the Pilgrim   38

4. The Pilgrim's Compass—Encounter   57

5. The Pilgrim's Compass—Struggle   70

6. The Pilgrim's Compass—Wounding,
   Wilderness, Wandering   82

7. The Pilgrim's Compass—New Name   98

8. Pilgrimage as an Anticipation
   of the Eighth Day   107

   Notes   111

ACKNOWLEDGMENTS

This book grows out of my work with the adult faith-formation ministry called the Pilgrimage (https://www.thepilgrimage.net), which is being developed at First Presbyterian Church in Fargo, North Dakota. Nearly everything I know about pilgrimage has been learned in the years that the Pilgrimage has been in development. My fellow pilgrims at First Presbyterian Church in Fargo, as well as at Shallowford Presbyterian Church in Lewisville, North Carolina (where the Pilgrimage is also being implemented), have been my teachers, and I am so very glad that we have been on the path to a Spirit-led and joyful discipleship together.

I have also had the help of a group of trusted readers whose feedback on this book from its earliest drafts has proven invaluable in the process of clarifying my thoughts and improving my writing. I offer my great gratitude to these readers who have read multiple drafts and faithfully responded with feedback: Coni Clark, Frances Dillie, Colleen Ford-Dunker, Melanie Hammond Clark, Jane Hubbard, Sarah Lang, Kit O'Neill, Janet Sockwell, and Ann Ulliman.

Tom Taylor, Joseph Small, and the entire board of the Institute of Church Renewal have all been incredibly supportive and encouraging as I undertook the work of writing this book. Tom and Joe were the ones who initially encouraged me to think of writing on the subject of pilgrimage, and I will be forever grateful for their friendship and assistance.

I must also say a brief word in memoriam for two pivotal influences on my pilgrimage of faith. Though both of these fellow pilgrims had gone on to join the saints in the light by the time I began writing, they nevertheless have been my constant companions on the path of completing this book. I met Ben Campbell Johnson in 1988 as I arrived at Columbia Theological Seminary to begin my studies. Ben was one of those faculty members who consistently gave me the impression that he had recently talked with God. He, of course, would have demurred had I said that to him. I found his deep faith and profound love of the church to be expressed in humble labors. His way of living the faith inspired me over the decades as our friendship grew. Though in my estimation (and the estimation of the many who were influenced by his books and teaching) he was a great person of faith and a disciple whose life we could aspire to emulate, Ben consistently and humbly insisted that God was at work in us all and that we would do well to find our own path of fidelity with God—a path that would be uniquely shaped by our own gifts and graces. I often have Ben in mind as I make pilgrimage, and I have written this book, in part, in loving memory of this dear friend and trusted mentor.

I also desire to mention in memoriam my mother, Rita McKerley Lang. My mother was one of those people who teach the faith not by telling so much as by living. In the final decades of her life she devoted more and more of her time and considerable talents to her own growth as a disciple of Jesus. More than that, she dedicated herself to the growing and supporting of other disciples in the church.

Her wisdom in knowing when to speak and when to remain silent, when to intervene and when to let others learn by experience, and her profound trust that God held both her and those she loved in God's grace are an example to me and have deeply shaped my own journey.

Finally, Abraham sojourned with Sarah, Jacob sojourned with Leah and Rachel, Moses wandered with his siblings Aaron and Miriam, and for more than thirty years I have made my journey of faith with Sarah, my beloved wife and friend. We have been on multiple pilgrimages to places throughout Europe and the Holy Land, as well as sojourning in the way a pastor and spouse must when hearing and responding to the call to serve in distant places. Twice now we have been called to go more than a thousand miles away from her family, and both times she has said yes to the move without complaint. Sarah's willingness to yield to the demands to "go" when the call came is a marvel and a blessing to me. She has been my faithful fellow pilgrim through all the moments of life—in joy and in sorrow, in sickness and in health, for richer and for poorer—and I am so very glad that we have made this journey together. Our sons, Daniel and Benjamin, are at the leaping-off point where their journeys are beginning to diverge from our own. Though we are separated by many miles, I know that they sojourn within the gaze and grace of God, and for that I give thanks.

PHL
Ordinary Time, Week 11
June 18, 2018

Chapter 1

PILGRIMAGE AND THE EMERGING CHURCH

You shall love the Lord your God with all your heart, and
with all your soul, and with all your strength, and with all
your mind; and your neighbor as yourself.
                                        —Luke 10:27

There we have it: a simple command to govern our life
before God. Love God with all our heart, soul, mind, and
strength—and love our neighbor as ourself. Not a one of
the elements of this imperative requires the participation of
the neighbor. All of this can be accomplished in the transformation of a person's heart from calculating rigidity to
compassionate self-giving. Indeed, one can argue that all of
the instructions of Scripture, from the law given at Sinai to
the new commandment entrusted to the disciples by Jesus,
aim at the creation of a workable human community gov-
erned by the demands of love and justice. Jesus gave us the
commandment to "make disciples of all nations, baptizing
them in the name of the Father and of the Son and of the
Holy Spirit, and teaching them to obey everything that I
have commanded you" (Matt. 28:19–20), and yet, the question persists—how shall we go about "making disciples"?
How do those of us who are dedicated to the vision of a
workable human community of love and justice work with
God in achieving the goal? And more precisely, how are we
to think about helping *others* to become what they are supposed to be? The temptation is to begin by attempting to
change others—to seek to shape them in our (presumably)
more Christlike image.

We, of course, would not be the first to attempt this.

It is precisely this sort of activity that leads the apostle Paul, in his first letter to the church at Corinth, to warn about the dangers of one person in the body of Christ insisting that another person in the body be like themselves. The ear should stop telling the eye to be an ear, he argues, because God has arranged the human community analogously to a body, whose many cooperating parts all belong but are radically different from one another (1 Cor. 12).

My own exploration of the discipline of pilgrimage stems from my desire to love God with all my heart, soul, strength, and mind, and to love my neighbors as I believe God loves them by working to establish a human community of love and justice. I am also convinced that the apostle Paul is on to something when he advises the early church to recognize *both* (a) that they belong to one another in profound and mutually supporting ways (as a body of Christ), *and* (b) that each of them individually should resist the urge to insist that other parts of the body conform to their own experience of faith (an ear should not to be measured by its capacity to be an eye). We are to work out *our own* salvation (Phil. 2:12).

There is good evidence that the earliest Christians heard this advice from Jesus and Paul and got busy taking it to heart. They recognized how much work was needed to transform their own hardened hearts, and they eschewed the need to attend to the sins of others. Abba Moses offers a typically acerbic comment:

> It is folly for a man who has a dead person in his house to leave him there and go to weep over his neighbour's dead.[1]

Or again, in the sayings of the desert fathers:

A brother asked the same old man, "How does the fear of God dwell in the soul?" The old man said, "If a man is possessed of humility and poverty, and if he does not judge others, the fear of God will come to him."[2]

More recently we have this observation:

The colossal misunderstanding of our time is the assumption that insight will work with people who are unmotivated to change. If you want your child, spouse, client, or boss to shape up, stay connected while changing yourself rather than trying to fix them.[3]

As we make our way into the twenty-first century, many are looking for an expression of discipleship that speaks meaningfully to Christians in our time. There is a yearning among people of faith for a discipleship that is at one and the same time more personally intimate and relevant and also grows out of and nurtures authentic Christian community. We yearn to follow the apostle Paul's admonition to "work out [our] own salvation with fear and trembling," and at the same time to form authentic Christian community by building up one another through encouragement and love. To prosper in the next era, the Christian church must find an appropriate balance between *individual experiences of transformation* and the equally critical task of *living in and cultivating a workable human community*.

In recent years I have been exploring the metaphor and practice of pilgrimage as a tool for faith formation in individual disciples and also as a source of renewal and revitalization of the church as a whole. I am growing in confidence that the church will be renewed in the power of the Spirit as individuals embrace again the ancient practice of pilgrimage, both as metaphor for the daily walk of discipleship and also as an intentional journey of faith that uses prayerful travel to assist an inner transformation. This is where the concepts of pilgrim and pilgrimage are useful. As anthropologists Victor and Edith Turner have observed, "At the heart of pilgrimage is the folk, the ordinary people who choose a 'materialist' expression of their religion."[4] One does not need advanced theological training to respond to the impulse to set out on a journey with God—a journey in which both the kinesis and the ordinary aspects of life become saturated with meaning and depth. Life is experienced as a peregrination[5] prompted by the presence of the Spirit which perpetually calls us out of our settled places and into a wild adventure with God. The Pilgrimage ministry and this volume about the pilgrim's compass are meant to aid in the emergence of a renewed and vibrant community of faith which has as its goal that we "learn to hear the call of God and respond in faith, journeying together with friends on the path to a Spirit-led and joyful life."[6] What follows is my modest contribution to the ongoing dialogue about faith formation in the twenty-first century and the impact of forming serious and passionate people of faith for the renewal of the church.

THE EARLY CHURCH, THE CONSTANTINIAN CHURCH, AND THE CHURCH OF THE TWENTY-FIRST CENTURY

To better consider how this call to pilgrimage impacts the current church, it will be helpful to consider a history of the church and its place in society. Since the church became the darling of the empire (beginning in the early fourth century with the support of the emperor Constantine) it has struggled with the seemingly inevitable consequences of being so closely aligned with the halls of power. Empires and empire-dependent churches feel a strong impulse to maintain the status quo. After all, the status quo is the circumstance that has them in ascendance. Empires maintain the status quo by exerting their will upon the subjects of the empire through military/police presence and taxation. Churches maintain the status quo by asserting that they are the final possessors and arbiters of *truth*. When an empire can deploy *power* and its churches can assert the certitude of *truth*, it is a forceful combination. The ascendance of the Christian church in the empires that arose around the Mediterranean basin in the fourth century is well documented, and the mighty combination of power and certitude that the so-called Constantinian church[7] wielded perhaps explains its remarkable resilience. For roughly sixteen hundred years the Christian church has enjoyed a position of privilege in the empires of Europe and, later, the Americas.

But this marriage of church and state has never been without its critics. It is not a coincidence that the great abbas and ammas (fathers and mothers) of the early Christian monastic movements were fleeing from the society of the empire and from the churches that served the empire at almost exactly the same time as the church was coming into its newfound position of privilege. These devout women and men took up residence in the deserts of the Thebaid.[8] They left a church and a culture dominated by those who were successful, in favor of a simple life dedicated to the pursuit of God. In eschewing a life of faith dominated by an ascendant church in an ascendant empire, they were abandoning also the impulse to maintain the status quo. Though they did not themselves use this term, I believe that the faith they hoped to preserve—the faith they had inherited from the Christians of the first centuries—could be better described as a faith of the *status viatoris*.[9] They honored the impulse to allow their feet to walk on unfamiliar paths and their eyes to behold unfamiliar scenes because they had heard an invitation from God to "go." They became wayfarers and wanderers for the love of God—trusting that, by God's grace, they were becoming someone new, or rather that they were becoming the truest expression of themselves.

The earliest Christians existed as a small subset of the overall population, and they had modest expectations of their capacity to rule (or even substantively change) the empire in which they lived. There were no illusions about creating a "Christian nation" in those early years. Discipleship focused on the possibility that in each and every moment a person could be present and aware of the reality of God and responsive to the demands of living in synergy with God's will. One was to be faithful in the moment, yielding to the demands of love, and then trust that God was engaged to complete great works of transformation in the larger society. And there is more. It was a discipleship far more focused on what one *did* (orthopraxy) than on the orthodoxy of one's thoughts. A faithful life was somatic (embodied) and as available to the layperson as to the priest because it had not yet become the wordy and excessively intellectual faith that maintaining the status quo would require.

After the Christian church became an official religion of the state, it was natural that it would begin to think of itself as the sort of institution that should devise great plans for the conversion of an unbelieving population and the transformation of the broader culture into a Christian culture. For many hundreds of years (roughly 380 CE to the late twentieth century) the institutional church saw itself either as a rival for political power or as a partner in civic transformation. The needs of the empire for good citizens can easily be confused with the needs of a dominant faith for good communicants. Faith formation then begins to take the form of civic and ecclesiological indoctrination whose goal is not transformed and joyful discipleship as much as compliant members of church and state. Both the process for producing such Christians and the goal of these ways of making disciples stand in significant contrast to the patterns we find in, for example, the faith formation of the desert communities of the early centuries of the Christian faith. The faith formation of those pre-Constantinian communities of faith relied heavily on solitude, silence, prayer (both public and private), and individual transformation.

Now, as the twenty-first century begins, it seems clear that whatever position of privilege and power the church once had, its current influence is much diminished. It is a shrinking circle of Christians who continue to hope that the United States will be a "Christian nation" again—at least in the sense of being a nation in which Christianity has an unrivaled level of hegemony and influence. The steady decline in membership experienced by nearly every Christian tradition in the United States in recent decades is but one barometer of the changing circumstances in which the church must find a new way to minister faithfully in a hurting world.

From *Resident Aliens*, published nearly thirty years ago, to *The Benedict Option: A Strategy for Christians in a Post-Christian Nation*, published in 2017,[10] a number of scholars have suggested that it is time for the church to rethink its sense of self in light of the shifting position of the church in the structures of power and influence within society. I believe that the Constantinian church, with its focus on delivering certitudes designed to support the status quo, is poorly situated to provide opportunities that speak convincingly to Christians in a post-Constantinian world. When the church was small and outside the circles of political influence, it was easier to see that the locus of transformation in faith belonged to each individual disciple. Discipleship by its nature happens one heart, one person of faith at a time. While community can provide structure and opportunity for discipleship to grow, discipleship is by its nature humble and simple and not easily orchestrated from the top down.

Sixteen centuries of Christian privilege in the governance of empires perhaps led the church to a place of hubris that confused *our plans* with *God's plans*. If, in humility, we acknowledge that we cannot know with clarity God's big plans for the transformation of the world, the locus of our attention for the task of "making disciples" shrinks back again within the circle of an individual's life before God. We return to something closer to those opening centuries when one was to be faithful in the moment, yielding to the demands of love, and then one trusted God to complete great works of transformation in oneself and in the larger society too.

The church emerging in the opening decades of the twenty-first century is a smaller church with a less obvious impact on the social structures of the dominant culture. And yet this smaller church, fewer in number, is increasingly made up of those for whom a vibrant faith is woven into every aspect of life. What some view as "decline" in the church, as the numbers of active members and the dollars they contribute become smaller, others view as the church returning to a way of being church and individuals returning to a way of being disciples that has many points of resonance with the Christians of the early centuries of the faith.

In the twenty-first century one must choose to live as a person of faith for reasons that are not culturally supported. One can no longer assume that the neighbors will be attending church or that the local sports programs will honor one's need to attend Lord's Day worship. The cost of discipleship is increasingly like the cost of discipleship prior to the emergence of the Constantinian church, when Christians lived as a small minority in societies that did not understand or support them. In the first centuries of the faith, the surrounding culture viewed the Christians mostly with indifference, and occasionally with hostility. I am not suggesting that we live under the kind of religious intolerance that sadly delivered some of those early Christian communities to the violence of martyrdom—only that we have entered a historical era in which people choose the faith for increasingly personal reasons.

The overly intellectual and conflict-driven nature of the mainline church of the late twentieth century[11] is being replaced by a church filled with those who are increasingly disinterested in passing judgment on their neighbor and also increasingly hungry for a vibrant relationship with the living "persons" of the Trinity.[12] This too connects with the faith of the early centuries, when, for example, the desert mothers and fathers taught that a life of unceasing prayer and communion with God led one to have a heart of compassion and to refuse to make judgments about the relative merit of one's neighbors. Abba Moses, for example, advises believers to bear your own faults and not to pay attention to anyone else wondering whether they are good or bad. . . . Do not think anything bad in your heart towards anyone. . . . Do not have hostile feelings towards anyone and do not let dislike dominate your heart.[13]

Finally, in the church beginning to emerge now, the renewal of faith and vision among laity is the driving force. The Spirit is powerfully at work in the hunger that is driving more and more laypeople to seek out a meaningful and vibrant relationship with God. As one layperson wrote not long ago, "I have been in the church my whole life, but I must confess that only now am I setting out on a journey of faith to see if I can come to love the God I have known about all my life—but never loved."[14]

This renewal happens from the ground up, one heart at a time, and is not much in the control of pastors and judicatories. And yet, the larger church and its leaders can play an important and helpful role in the emerging church by providing space and support for the renewal of faith among those in whom the Spirit is so powerfully at work.

THE BIBLE AND PILGRIMAGE

When early Christians turned to Scripture, they found a complex narrative of God and God's people. That narrative begins with God shaping those whom God has called through pilgrimage. Adam and Eve depart the garden. Cain is left to wander east of Eden. Abram and Sarai depart Haran and wander the better part of a lifetime (south through the Negev and back to Canaan) in search of the place where

God would bless them. Jacob departs Canaan and sojourns to Haran (and back) on his way to Shechem. Moses departs Egypt for Sinai, only to return and lead the exodus of God's people in search of the promised land. The patterns are repeated in the New Testament narratives. The Gospel of Matthew moves Joseph, Mary, and Jesus from Bethlehem to Egypt and back to Galilee. Peter leaves Jerusalem for Joppa, only to be led by the Spirit to Caesarea and back. Not surprisingly, Jesus often invites new disciples with the imperative, "Follow me." Again and again biblical faith is shaped and transformed by the practice of journeying in response to God's call—pilgrimage.

Faith involves the daily decision to arise again and follow after the one who calls us. Though this daily practice of setting out in faith often occurs in the mundane elements of life, it is punctuated by places and times when God is encountered in particularly vivid and transforming ways (Jacob's ladder, Moses' burning bush, Peter's vision at Joppa). Faith as pilgrimage is thus both the *daily practice of discipleship* and the *journey to a place of hope-filled and expectant encounter.* Never is this dual nature of pilgrimage more clearly apparent than in the forty-year peregrination of the people of Israel as they wander from Egypt in search of the land of promise. They are going somewhere specific, but that pilgrimage to the promised land is lived existentially in the daily grind of desert wandering.

For Christians, the practice of sojourning with God is a discipline of emulating our Lord, who himself discloses that our God is a pilgrim God. When we recite the Nicene Creed and profess, "For us and for our salvation he came down from heaven, was incarnate of the Holy Spirit and the Virgin Mary and became truly human," we are describing a God who left God's "home" in order to make sojourning among us God's pilgrimage. It is not surprising that pilgrimage seems always to have been a part of Christian religious practice.

A *BRIEF* HISTORY OF CHRISTIAN PILGRIMAGE

From its earliest writings we see that the Christian community was aware that the sites of various stories about Jesus could be of import to those who followed after. Origen (ca. 184–253 CE), in his voluminous writings on Scripture, initiated a style of exegesis that included details pointing to sites relating to biblical narratives. Eusebius (ca. 260–339) created a biblical gazetteer during his own exploration of the biblical region.[15] Eusebius is known to have had a large collection of Origen's works and likely built upon them in assembling his guide. These early writings of the Christian corpus show that from the early centuries of the faith, the places connected with Scripture were already being identified and preserved, presumably to aid those who would seek to visit them as an element of their faith formation.

Early in the fourth century, Queen Helena (250–330), mother of Constantine the Great, made pilgrimage to the Holy Land and established a church in Bethlehem as well as on the Mount of Olives in Jerusalem. Egeria, a nun from a monastery most likely in Spain, provides the earliest extant written account of pilgrimage to the Holy Land.[16] Egeria made her pilgrimage roughly from 381 to 384. Augustine of Hippo describes his discipleship as "pilgrimage," as does Gregory of Nazianzus.[17]

Pilgrimage continued as a practice of Christian devotion, reaching great popularity in the Middle Ages. Though early Protestant Reformers criticized the misuse of pilgrimage in the church of the late Middle Ages, a review of the writings of Martin Luther, John Calvin, William Tyndale, Thomas More, Thomas Cranmer, and others reveals that those early voices of the Protestant Reformation were inclined to see pilgrimage as a powerful and biblical metaphor for discipleship. They all allowed, if somewhat grudgingly, that even travel pilgrimage (when properly practiced) could be useful for faith formation.

Luther, for example, was concerned about people who neglected their duties to those at home in a feverish rush to go on some spiritual flight of fancy. He writes:

> Those whom God has commanded a man to keep in body and soul he leaves behind, and wants to serve God in some place or another, some thing that was never commanded. No bishop forbids and no preacher rebukes such a perverse practice. In fact, in the interests of their own covetousness the clergy endorse such practices. Every day they think up more and more pilgrimages.[18]

This is a reasonable concern. If we take our leave to go on pilgrimage in a way that unduly inconveniences others or, worse, causes harm to those God has entrusted to our care, then clearly our travel is of an unholy kind.

Calvin, for his part, seems to view travel pilgrimage as problematic. In his commentary on Acts 14:15 he lists the worship of dead men's bones as a typical form of idolatry. Indeed, throughout his commentary on Scripture he insists that the outward expression of faith must match inner fidelity and obedience. Commenting on Scripture decrying the distance between outward act and inward integrity, he writes:

> And thus, if a monk rise from the bed of his adultery to chant a few psalms without one spark of godliness in his breast, or if a whore-monger, a thief, or any foresworn villain, seeks to make reparation for his crimes by mass or pilgrimage, they would be loath to consider this lost labor. By God, on the other hand, such a disjunction of the form from the inward sentiment of devotion is branded as sacrilege.[19]

And yet, in the *Institutes* Calvin acknowledges that the apostle Paul taught that those who follow Christ "must be pilgrims in the world, that we may not fail of obtaining the heavenly inheritance."[20]

William Tyndale, the great contributor to English Bible translation, suggests that as long as Christians have met all of their moral duties at home, it is permissible for them to go on pilgrimage. He writes in response to Thomas More's *Dialogue*:

> To speak of pilgrimages, I say, that a christian man, so that he leave nothing undone at home that he is bound to do, is free to go whither he will; only after the doctrine of the Lord, whose servant he is, and not his own. . . . If he go to this or that place, to hear a sermon, or because his mind is not quiet at home; or if, because his heart is too much occupied on his worldly businesses, by reason of occasions at home, he get him into a more quiet and still place, where his mind is more abstract, and pulled from worldly thoughts, it is well done. And in all these places, if whatsoever it be, whether lively preaching, ceremony, relic, or image, stir up his heart to God . . . that he thither go, I am content.[21]

The biblical basis for pilgrimage is clear, the evidence of its place in the spiritual disciplines of the church is copious, and its practice, which had been in decline in recent centuries, is once again resurgent, as can be seen in the nearly hundredfold increase in pilgrims who have completed the Camino de Santiago de Compostela in recent decades.[22] People of faith in many different circumstances appear to be hearing, "Go from your country and your kindred and your father's house to the land that I will show you. I will make of you a great nation, and I will bless you, and make your name great, so that you will be a blessing" (Gen. 12:1–2) as a word befitting them personally.

In the following pages I define pilgrimage and explain why it is an especially relevant and powerful spiritual discipline for individuals and communities of faith in the twenty-first century. I also explore the pilgrim's compass as a tool that can be usefully deployed in one's faith formation both in the daily task of discipleship and on those occasions when one feels the call to leave home in pursuit of God in the wider world.

QUESTIONS FOR REFLECTION AND DISCUSSION

1. The story of Moses and the people of God escaping Egypt and making a forty-year journey through the wilderness to the promised land is a good example of pilgrimage as *both* a daily commitment to discipleship *and* an adventure with God aimed at liberation and new life. Where can you see these two aspects of pilgrimage at work in your life today?

2. For more than three hundred years, the early Christians lived as a small minority within the empire. They

were often ignored and overlooked, and occasionally disdained. Some historians see a parallel between the experiences of the early Christians and the current circumstance of the church in the twenty-first century. Do you see a parallel? Why or why not?

3. There is a resurgence of interest in the discipline of pilgrimage. The number of Christians who set out in pursuit of God has grown year by year in recent decades. Why do you think this ancient practice is growing in popularity again? What brings you to read about pilgrimage and the pilgrim's compass?

JOURNALING AND PRAYER EXERCISES

1. The beginning of a call to pilgrimage is often felt in restlessness and longing to "go": the push of restlessness with your current circumstance, and the pull of feeling that God has a blessing for you "out there" somewhere. Spend time in your journal or prayers reflecting on the call to pilgrimage. What is pushing and what is pulling you?

2. In chapter 1, Abba Moses counsels us to pay attention to our own faults and to stop paying attention to the faults of others. He urges that we stop letting dislike dominate us. Spend time journaling and/or praying about the place of judgment in your spiritual life. Do you find it hard to follow Abba Moses's counsel? Are there activities or sources of information in your life that lead you to focus on what you dislike? How might you avoid letting dislike dominate your life?

SUGGESTED BOOKS FOR FURTHER READING

Rod Dreher, *The Benedict Option: A Strategy for Christians in a Post-Christian Nation* (New York: Penguin Random House, 2017).

William Harmless, SJ, *Desert Christians: An Introduction to the Literature of Early Monasticism* (New York: Oxford University Press, 2004).

Scott H. Hendrix, *Early Protestant Spirituality*, Classics of Western Spirituality (New York: Paulist Press, 2009).

Thomas Merton, *The Wisdom of the Desert* (New York: New Directions Books, 1960).

Jonathan Sumption, *The Age of Pilgrimage: The Medieval Journey to God* (Mahwah, NJ: Hidden Spring, 2003).

Brent Webb-Mitchell, *School of the Pilgrim: An Alternative Path to Christian Growth* (Louisville, KY: Westminster John Knox Press, 2007).

Chapter 2

PILGRIMAGE AS THE HOME OF OUR SOJOURNING

Each day is a journey and the journey itself home.
—Matsuo Bashō[1]

TOWARD A DEFINITION OF PILGRIMAGE

In recent years as I have led a number of travel pilgrimages, I have often been asked to define pilgrimage and, more specifically, to speak to the two most common notions of pilgrimage:

1. Travel to a distant location for religious purposes
2. Pilgrimage as a metaphor for discipleship throughout one's life

Over the years I have collected dozens of attempts to succinctly define pilgrimage from authors across the centuries who have given us a variety of ideas about this discipline. I find something of value in each of them, but none of these efforts capture the full essence of the practice of pilgrimage. Nearly every definition is aimed at one of the two notions listed above, which is also the distinction my fellow pilgrims are often interested in sorting out. Is pilgrimage a commitment to lifelong discipleship, a metaphor for shaping one's life before God? Or is it the act of making a specific trip in search of a better love for God and one's neighbors? It is, of course, both.

Interestingly, the Hebrew word translated "pilgrim"

or "pilgrimage" has connotations appropriate to both of these main definitions. The word is *magor* (pronounced "maw-goor´"),[2] and it derives from a word for "dwelling" or "home" but morphs in its usage to mean something like "place of sojourning." Thus we have the odd juxtaposition of the word for home with the practice of sojourning. Perhaps the best and most intriguing use of the word is in Psalm 119:54, where the Hebrew is *bet meguray* (pronounced "bet´ maw-goor'ay")[3] or "house/home of our sojourning/wandering." I love the oxymoronic tension of this phrase—the *home* of my *wandering/sojourning*. In Hebrew, "pilgrimage" suggests a tension within the very root of the words used to describe it. The foci are:

1. Home, a residence
2. Wandering or sojourning

We find the same tension in the practice of pilgrimage both as a metaphor for faithful discipleship all our days and as travel for the purpose of sacred encounter. To be a pilgrim is thus to *inhabit the home of our sojourning*. In common parlance, one is *either* at home *or* sojourning. When the psalmist says, "Your statutes have been my songs wherever I make the house of my sojourning" (Ps. 119:54, au. trans.), we imagine the life of people like Abraham and Sarah, the wandering Arameans[4] whose faith-testing adventures with God initiate the history of the biblical patriarchs and matriarchs.

We pilgrims are left to embody the mystery that we inhabit the most natural and authentic of things (our true home) by escaping the familiar confines of our "home." We pass over the threshold of our domicile and seek out our risen Lord in the wilderness of the world. And if Genesis

12 is to be trusted, we do that understanding that God will reward our courage and obedience by blessing us and by entrusting to us the noble work of being God's blessing to those we meet along the way. Below I explore pilgrimage as a way of describing our discipleship when we are at home, and then as a practice of spiritual formation as we sojourn on a travel pilgrimage.

DOMESTIC PILGRIMAGE

Much of our faith formation happens in a domestic context. We live out our faith more often at home than away. There is a moment in Genesis when Jacob describes the breadth of his whole life and of his ancestors' lives—"the days of my pilgrimage" and "the days of their sojourning"—with the word *magor* (author translation).[5] As noted above, *magor* is derived from a word for "dwelling" or "home." Jacob, in remembering both his story and the story of his ancestors, sees both wandering and settling as aspects of their sojourning/pilgrimage. To refer to all of life as the days of his pilgrimage is to acknowledge the ways in which pilgrimage functions as a metaphor for daily faithful living.

Ever since Jesus indicated to his disciples that the Father's house has "many dwelling places" and that he was going before to "prepare a place" for them (John 14:2), his followers have understood that we are a people in search of our true home. The Pilgrimage ministry captures this longing in one stanza of its Pilgrim's Prayer:

> Lead us, Lord,
> by the restlessness of spiritual longing,
> by the hope of finding our true home,

by the yearning of a hungry heart.
Lord, hear our prayer.

I am a homebody. I like being at home, and even
when I travel to beautiful places and enjoy myself, I more
or less continually yearn for home. That has applied to my
connection to my faith community too. Born into a family
that attended a Presbyterian church, it was my inclination
to stay "home" within the familiar confines of my tradition.
There is, of course, wisdom in making a commitment to stability, choosing to remain within a religious tradition long
enough to fully plumb the depths of what it offers before
flitting off to some new religious experience. Anthony, the
father of monks, advised in the early fourth century:

> Pay attention to what I tell you: whoever you may be,
> always have God before your eyes; whatever you do,
> do it according to the testimony of the holy Scrip-
> tures; in whatever place you live, do not easily leave
> it. Keep these three precepts and you will be saved.[6]

Staying at home in one's community provides opportunities for growth that cannot be found when one leaves
every time there is discomfort. Thus Anthony's counsel, "in
whatever place you live, do not easily leave it." This pref-
erence for stability was eventually included in the Rule of
St. Benedict, and it has had a profound influence on the
development of Western monasticism. I am a Presbyterian
pastor, not a monastic, but it is easy for me to see the value
of stability in my own ministry, both for myself and in the
lives of those I seek to serve.

For most of us, the experience of our religious life
is that our discipleship is practiced amid the quotidian

tasks of brushing our teeth, cleaning the house, running the errands that keep the family going, and completing our work—whatever that looks like. This stable location for much of our growth as disciples is not a bad thing. At home, we embrace the challenging demands of our discipleship to love our family, our neighbors, our colleagues at work, and our fellow Christians at church. Staying at home and attending to the taxing and virtuous task of loving those closest to us is an essential aspect of any serious life of faith.

I am the child of a surgeon who left for the hospital in the dark hours of morning and who often returned home in the darkness of the evening. He was obviously very competent at work, where he served as chief of staff in addition to his other duties, but he was seldom home. He died when I was twelve years old, before he and I were able to develop a deep and strong relationship. Years later, when I had become a father of two small sons, I called my mother one afternoon in exasperation. I was tired, had work to do, and was at home watching the boys in the afternoons while my wife taught violin. My job was to get the boys out of the house so they would not interrupt my wife's teaching. I described to my mother how hard it was for me to be a primary caregiver to my toddler and infant sons and how I would rather be at church doing what I thought was more important work. My mother listened for a long time and then said simply, "Paul, your boys will have more time one-on-one with you this year than you had with your father in your whole life. I know how hard this is for you, but you need to stay home and learn how to be a father to them." It was profoundly good advice and could have come from the Christian mothers and fathers of the fourth century. Being at home and learning there to live faithfully for God is an essential part of the pilgrimage of faith.

Our discipleship and the community that supports our faith can be powerfully deployed to address some of the great troubles of our age. Sociologist and Lutheran theologian Peter Berger has written convincingly about the "homeless mind" suffered by many who are dislocated by the rapid pace of modern change.[7] Jewish theologian Michael Fishbane has written more recently of the ways our communities of faith help us to maintain mindfulness in a mindless world.[8] In a world prone to destructive forms of homelessness and endless distractions leading to mindlessness, knowing who we are and where we belong is a great blessing to people of faith.

In recent years, as I have witnessed the growing practice of pilgrimage as a discipline of faith, I have found myself thinking that Peter Berger was on to something when he suggested that one of the casualties of modernity is that people are increasingly "homeless." Perhaps the rise in the practice of pilgrimage stems from the bewildering disorientation felt by so many who find themselves "in a distant country" of rapid technological change and societal upheaval. Perhaps we pilgrims are waking up to our dislocation from our true home and we are setting out on a somatic peregrination aimed at returning to our Father's house. We are dislodged from the home we thought we knew and step out in hope that God will show us where we belong. It is one of those holy and divine ironies that we must leave home in order to truly know home. As usual, it is the poets who know the truth of this best. In 1942, T. S. Eliot wrote:

> We shall not cease from exploration
> And the end of all our exploring
> Will be to arrive where we started
> And know the place for the first time.[9]

Walter Brueggemann, too, has written of the place of land in the story of Israel as a tension between home and homelessness:

> Whereas pursuit of space may be a flight from history, a yearning for a place is a decision to enter history with an identifiable people in an identifiable pilgrimage. Humanness, as biblical faith promises it, will be found in belonging to and referring to that locus in which the peculiar historicity of a community has been expressed and to which recourse is made for purposes of orientation, assurance, and empowerment.[10]

Brueggemann goes on to point out that the people of Israel are also homeless people. The call that initiates the formation of Israel begins, "Go from your country and your kindred and your father's house" (Gen. 12:1). What makes this homelessness productive rather than destructive is that it is chosen.

> The sojourn is freely chosen, not imposed. It is a choice made by those who could have chosen not to leave. The choice means to throw one's self totally on Yahweh, not in order to live in some nonhistorical relation with God but to be led to a better place, one characterized by promises not known either in Ur or in one's father's house.[11]

Describing a life of faith using the metaphor of pilgrimage is common in Christian literature. The Cappadocian, Father Gregory of Nazianzus (ca. 330–ca. 389), hoped that if he was remembered for anything it would be that he lived his life as a pilgrimage in Christ:

Yet may my only honour be that which is in God, and
may my pilgrimage and my home be in Christ Jesus
our Lord, to Whom, with the Father and the Holy
Ghost, be glory for ever. Amen.[12]

Augustine of Hippo (354–430) writes of the breadth
of his life in faith as pilgrimage:

This is the fruit of my confessions, not of what I was,
but of what I am, that I may confess this not before
Thee only, in a secret exultation with trembling, and
a secret sorrow with hope, but in the ears also of the
believing sons of men,—partakers of my joy, and shar-
ers of my mortality, my fellow-citizens and the companions of my pilgrimage, those who are gone before,
and those that are to follow after, and the comrades
of my way.[13]

We find a long-standing pattern in the Christian tradition of thinking of life's sojourn as a pilgrimage made in
the context of living as faithfully as one can as a disciple
of Jesus. Understood this way, our pilgrimage in faith
includes the many mundane habits and practices that
surround simple discipleship: daily prayer, Bible study,
worship attendance, and involvement with the many ministry opportunities provided by the church and the larger
community. One never needs to leave the confines of one's
neighborhood to fully engage in this aspect of pilgrimage.

Life has a way of presenting us with opportunities
to practice aspects of sojourning even when at home. We
celebrate the birth of a child, and immediately our world is
turned topsy-turvy as we lose sleep comforting the colicky
baby and discover a new balance in family life. An elderly
parent grows ill, and we make the bewildering transition

from child to caregiver. We lose employment and find that we are free from responsibilities of work but also free from the income those responsibilities provided, and we go out in search of our next vocation. These all require that we set out on a new journey of discovery, and they all could well happen while we remain at home.

Much can be gained by considering our daily discipleship at home as pilgrimage. Pilgrims are expectant people—they expect to encounter the risen Lord. For all of the benefits of faith grown at home, it is sometimes true that in familiar environs we lose that sense of expectancy. The very familiarity of our work and surroundings leads us to the conclusion that we have seen it all already, that our life has nothing surprising to offer. A daily practice of reminding ourselves that we are pilgrims can assist in awakening in us a newly invigorated attentiveness to the presence of God.

And there is more. When we consider our lifelong discipleship as a kind of pilgrimage, we are reminded of the ways in which our story is mysteriously interwoven with God's story. Daily discipleship is seen as our participation with God in the larger work of redemption that God is undertaking. We sojourn through this life recognizing that our journey with God is but a chapter in the larger story of God's work and that our wandering is not aimless, but is designed to bring us truly home.

TRAVEL PILGRIMAGE

I am sometimes asked about the need for travel pilgrimage. After all, it is pointed out, Jesus never commanded his disciples to make a pilgrimage. While it is true that none of the

Gospel accounts record Jesus urging pilgrimage by what he says, it is equally true that he surely urges pilgrimage by what he does. In what follows, we see the practice of pilgrimage in the biblical narrative and, more particularly, in the life of Jesus.

Years ago I was in a seminary course on the subject of Sabbath and Sabbath keeping. The first day, the instructor asked the class, "Why do we keep Sabbath?" A variety of answers came forth: because it is required by one of the Ten Commandments; because the weekend provides an easy way to do it; and so on. Eventually the instructor said, "*We keep Sabbath because God keeps Sabbath.*" It was the first time I connected the discipline I was attempting to establish in my life with the life of God—and that one observation immensely helped me to be a disciplined Sabbath-keeper.

One might say a similar thing about the discipline of pilgrimage. We are pilgrims, and we make our pilgrimages in emulation of God—who is a pilgrim God.

The first creedal statement in Scripture, which is in Deuteronomy, describes the pilgrimage of Abram and Sarai and their descendants:

> A wandering Aramean was my ancestor; he went down into Egypt and lived there as an alien, few in number, and there he became a great nation, mighty and populous. When the Egyptians treated us harshly and afflicted us, by imposing hard labor on us, we cried to the LORD, the God of our ancestors; the LORD heard our voice and saw our affliction, our toil, and our oppression. The LORD brought us out of Egypt with a mighty hand and an outstretched arm, with a terrifying display of power, and with signs

and wonders; and he brought us into this place and
gave us this land, a land flowing with milk and honey.
(Deut. 26:4–9)

When the Gospel of Matthew describes the early
life of Jesus, it is not surprising that he re-creates the journey to Egypt and back to the promised land (Matt. 2).
These various statements of faith and narratives that are
at the heart of our scriptural legacy describe an ellipti-
cal journey from home to a place at the margins and then
back homeward again. And yet, while our ancestors in
the faith return in a homeward direction, they often cannot return "home." Abram and Sarai do not return to Ur,
nor even to Haran. Jesus and his parents do not return to
Bethlehem, but instead settle in Nazareth. The peram-
bulations of pilgrimage seem to leave home as an elusive
destination.

The process of pilgrimage seems to naturally lean
toward the transitional, the provisional, the slightly uncertain. If home can be understood as the place for certitude
and settled assumptions, then pilgrimage is a sojourn in
the land of possibilities and hopes not yet fully realized. So
why would we choose the possibility and uncertainty of
pilgrimage over certainty? I think we choose pilgrimage for
love. Love of God, love of the others we will encounter, and
love of ourselves too. For it is love that gives birth to God's
pilgrimage among us. The incarnation of God in Jesus is
described by John's Gospel in this way:

And the Word became flesh and lived among us, and
we have seen his glory, the glory as of a father's only
son, full of grace and truth. . . . From his fullness we
have all received, grace upon grace. (John 1:14, 16)

It is God's grace-full impulse, an unmerited love for God's creatures, which brings God to us in the person of Jesus.

We too are drawn into pilgrimage by an impulse to love; journeying in search of a God we have known about our whole lives and whom we seek to love more fully; or perhaps to learn to love ourselves as God loves us; or maybe to learn to love all of God's children everywhere by sojourning among them and discovering that they too belong to God.

Luke's Gospel provides a compelling story about home and journeying to a distant place (15:11–32). Jesus tells the story of a man with two sons. The younger boy asks for his inheritance and, once he has it, leaves home to travel to a distant country where he squanders his resources in unhealthy living. He is reduced to feeding pigs and is so hungry himself that he wonders about eating the feed provided to the pigs. But there, in a distant land, Luke tells us he "came to himself," and he begins his journey back to the father.

Luke's story about the younger son presents the irony that it is in leaving his home and traveling a great distance that the young man comes to a place of clarity about his own identity. He leaves home presumably in search of something that is missing in his life, and once he is removed from the place and relationships that defined him he is able to freely embrace his true nature as a beloved child of the father. Only then is he able to begin the long journey back home.

Many of us who have spent many years growing as disciples in our homes, like the young man in Jesus' parable, are also aided in our pursuit of God by the practice of leaving home and journeying to a "distant country." That distant place may seem like the wilderness to us. Many years ago as I took my first call in a small town west of the Mississippi River, my brothers, who have a well-developed sense of humor, sent me a hand-drawn map that included only the states of the East Coast. Beyond the Mississippi there was only blank canvas and the warning, "There be beasties out there!" Travel pilgrimage by its nature takes us to the edges of our known world, and often that wilderness is just the right place for us to encounter God and be made new. That is exactly what happened when Sarah and I arrived in McGehee, Arkansas, to serve at First Presbyterian Church. We discovered good people who were serious about their faith and who took us in and loved us well beyond what we deserved. We were far from home, and the ways of the Mississippi delta were, perhaps at times, bewildering, but God was in the people among whom we sojourned, and we will forever remember them fondly. The time in McGehee also began to reshape me as a pastor and to help me see my own foibles and faults more clearly. A unique form of clarity can arise when we are in a new place and are able to practice self-examination apart from the many structures that normally define us.

When we travel as a pilgrimage, we are choosing to be bewildered. The Bible is full of stories in which people (including Jesus) encounter God in the wilderness. In fact, much of the story of God's history with God's people takes place in or at the edges of the wilderness. Biblical ideas about wilderness are unavoidably attached to the actual geographic wildernesses of the Jordan Rift Valley and the lands claimed by the people of God at the eastern end of the Mediterranean Sea. But in the biblical imagination, wilderness also is used as a metaphor for all manner of difficulties and experiences of marginalization and peril. It points to the unmapped and unknown, the place where one is concerned for food and shelter, where silence prevails in a wordy world, and where one is forced to give up the illusion of self-sufficiency and acknowledge one's utter dependence on God. The wilderness is where we choose to disconnect from the rat race in favor of a simpler, more grace-defined existence. The wilderness is the place where we are forced to encounter and deal with the limits of our capacity to control things. The author Belden Lane—after a year of watching his mother slowly die—went to the desert and wrote:

> Only at the periphery of our lives, where we and our understanding of God alike are undone, can we understand bewilderment as occasioning another way of knowing.[14]

Travel pilgrimage, a discipline that by its nature takes us away from the familiar and into the wilderness of the wider world, fosters that other way of knowing, which Lane suggests happens only at the periphery where our certitudes about ourselves, about our neighbors, and about God are undone. This aspect of pilgrimage can be seen in the decision to let go of our many certitudes and live into the mystery of our relationship with God. It is to choose curiosity over settled assumptions, and an ongoing dialogue (even disputation) with God over polite prayers that cost us nothing.

In my own experience with travel pilgrimage, one of the persistent struggles is to let the pilgrimage be what it is, rather than constantly measuring it by the yardstick of what I *expected* it to be. There is a danger for those who dream of going on a travel pilgrimage to, say, Jerusalem, or to Iona, or to some other well-known holy place, that we let our prayerful planning and faithful anticipation for the pilgrimage morph into a long list of expectations. We might, for example, expect to have a mountaintop experience of

divine epiphany where we find enlightenment. Or maybe
we expect that we will somehow achieve the status of holy
man or holy woman while on pilgrimage. Though I have
had moments of new and exciting clarity while on pilgrimage, and while I have occasionally been a more faithful
disciple than usual while walking the narrow streets of Jerusalem . . . it is far more often the case that my experience of
travel pilgrimage is one of making peace with the slippage
between what I hoped for and dreamed about versus what
actually happens.

In college I was in a very fine choir that toured every
spring. Dozens of us undergrads would pile into several
buses and caravan throughout the Southeast recruiting for
Furman University. It was a well-oiled machine of a trip
with teams of people assigned to every aspect of the logis-
tics. Each year, anticipating that the trip never goes according to plan, the director would tape a large poster board
to the front of every bus. It read simply, "Adjust, Adapt,
Accept." This became the mantra for our travel each April,
"adjust, adapt, accept." As I prepared to make a seven-week
pilgrimage to monasteries throughout Europe in 2008, one
of my parishioners made me a simple zipper pull for my day
bag with beads spelling, "Adjust, Adapt, Accept." It was a
message from God reminding me that the value of my travel
pilgrimage should not be determined by asking, "How well
did this trip produce the expected experiences?" Rather it
might be measured by asking, "How well did I look for God
in whatever circumstance the travel provided?"

I have spent years planning a trip and even employed
the assistance of professional guides at the destination, but
it is a near inevitability that things will (at some point) not
go according to plans. That is when a pilgrim has to be at
peace with the reality of the hard road of travel. We may

miss a meal or have less than our favorite kind of accommodations, or some cherished event will get canceled. In those moments we must ask, "Where is God in this?" and "What is it that the Spirit is trying to say to me right now?"

At the end of my 2008 sabbatical, after Sarah, our two boys, and I had trekked through Europe for seven weeks, we sat in a restaurant in downtown London and for several hours went around the circle answering questions like "What was the best moment for you?" and "What was the hardest moment?" "When did Dad lose it the worst?" "When did you learn something that you never knew before?" I eagerly wrote down everyone's answers, and those pages in my travel journal are a cherished possession now. They taught me that when we look back, we may see that some of the times when our pilgrimage seemed to go off the rails were when we grew the most.

INTEGRATED PILGRIMAGE

As noted above, it is tempting to think of pilgrimage as two distinct things:

1. A metaphor for the daily practice of faith, roughly synonymous with discipleship
2. A journey to a sacred destination or for a sacred purpose, made intentionally at a discrete time and place

While these distinctions at one level make sense and allow us to discuss pilgrimage as discipleship and travel pilgrimage with clarity, on another level the distinctions are unnecessary and may actually lead to misunderstanding. Pilgrimage is, in fact, both of these things coexisting at one and the same time. People are pilgrims as soon as they answer the call of God, even if that call never pulls them beyond the borders of their own home. And yet, the merits of heeding the impulse to travel out into the wilderness of the wide world in a reckless pursuit of God are also well documented, and many a pilgrim who begins with an indigenous faith finds over time that the longing of the heart pulls them out ever farther beyond familiar places. One can, as a disciple, be a pilgrim without ever traveling to any of the well-known and distant locations that have drawn people of faith for centuries. Yet most pilgrims will benefit from the unique struggles and blessings of participating in a travel pilgrimage.

Pilgrimage is a beautiful mystery. It is complexity within simplicity, and its refusal to be one thing has fascinated many Christian pilgrims from time immemorial. It is perhaps best understood to be a great many things existing in dynamic tension with one another.

On the one hand, for example, you need no esoteric knowledge to set out on pilgrimage. No degree in theology, no alignment with creedal orthodoxy is required. The discipline has always belonged to laypersons as much as or more than to theologians. It is a religious practice of ordinary folk in every age who hear God calling and who respond—oftentimes with little or no theological consideration or training. The mysteries of this discipline can be penetrated by simply practicing it with intention and reflecting on your life and experience as you go. And yet, on the other hand, for the pilgrim who desires to ponder, and who is inclined to ruminate on mysteries, the discipline of pilgrimage provides a lifetime's worth of material to consider. Pilgrims inclined to study and wonderment have well-worn guides in classics such as *The Way of the Pilgrim* and *Egeria's Travels* as well as a host of more modern books and resources about the practice of pilgrimage to feed the fire of their curiosity. Both the impulse to go without delay and the impulse to spend time in preparation have merits and demerits to consider. The pilgrim inclined to ponder must stop ruminating long enough to simply respond and go. The pilgrim inclined to race out the moment an impulse to go is felt does well to spend time in thoughtful and prayerful preparation.

For Reformed pilgrims, travel pilgrimage provides a rare opportunity to engage in a somatic spiritual practice. The Reformed tradition has often been so enamored with the power of words to carry theological freight, and so committed to the crafting of nuanced theological distinctions, that it has neglected embodied forms of devotion. Pilgrimage offers a way to regain a more balanced form of discipleship that honors both the intellect and the simple prayer of attentive movement. Thus pilgrimage is the marvelous nexus of an outward journey of faith connected to an inner odyssey of self-discovery.

As the title of this chapter suggests, I think that to be a pilgrim is to *inhabit the home of our sojourning.* Inhabiting the home of our sojourning is becoming the sort of disciple who is at home on the journey of faith. To wander through this world *with God* is to be never *lost.* It is to keep alive within us the wonder and fascination that accompanies travel—even when engaged with ordinary practices of life and faith at home. And it is to remain grounded and stable in our understanding of self—even when wandering the wider world for the love of God.

In the next chapter we will consider tools that can be used to guide us on our pilgrimage.

QUESTIONS FOR REFLECTION AND DISCUSSION

1. How does your spirit respond to the idea of your discipleship taking the form of perpetual sojourning?

2. Anthony advises, "in whatever place you live, do not easily leave it." Why do you think that he advises the discipline of stability? How might our decisions about church attendance and membership be changed if we heeded Anthony's counsel?

3. How might the practice of pilgrimage help you to be more mindful of the presence of God in your life?

4. How might pilgrimage, a discipline of leaving home, help you to find your true home and deepen the sense of home when you return?

5. The discipline of travel pilgrimage is to choose to be a stranger in a land not your own. Have you ever felt like a stranger? When traveling, have you realized that you do not know the native tongue of the people around you? How might God be encountered in the person of the stranger?

JOURNALING AND PRAYER EXERCISES

1. Think about a time in your life when you needed to relocate. Journal about that time, remembering what it was like to leave one home and create a new home. Ponder the ways that God was with you in the move and in the time that followed as you began a new chapter in life in a new place.

2. As a form of daily prayer, be on the lookout for God coming to you in the guise of a stranger. As you make your way through your ordinary daily tasks, keep yourself

open to the discovery that someone may be God's messenger to you.

3. A daily practice of reminding ourselves that we are pilgrims can assist in awakening in us a newly invigorated attentiveness to the presence of God. Incorporate this daily practice into your quiet or devotional time and journal about your awakened awareness and experiences of God, at home or on travel pilgrimage.

SUGGESTED BOOKS FOR FURTHER READING

Phil Cousineau, *The Art of Pilgrimage: The Seeker's Guide to Making Travel Sacred* (Newburyport, MA: Conari Press, 1998).

J. G. Davies, *Pilgrimage Yesterday and Today: Why? Where? How?* (London: SCM Press, 1988).

Edward C. Sellner, *Pilgrimage, Exploring a Great Spiritual Practice* (Notre Dame, IN: Sorin Books, 2004).

Chapter 3

NOT ALL WHO
WANDER ARE LOST:
TOOLS FOR THE PILGRIM

Chapter 1 introduced the subject and its relevance, and chapter 2 defined in more detail the concept of pilgrimage, using the phrase "home of our sojourning." This chapter offers tools for those who are "inhabiting the home of sojourning."

Maps or an atlas provide aid to those who wander. This chapter shows how the pilgrim's "atlas" combines the guidance offered by the Bible, life experience, the counsel of others, and a variety of tools, such as the Pilgrim's Prayer from the Pilgrimage ministry. It briefly introduces the compass, with a few words about cartography and the relatively modern arrival of the magnetic compass. Finally, I introduce the pilgrim's compass as a daily tool for orienting one's life toward God in pursuit of a transformed discipleship.

> Pilgrims are persons in motion—passing through territories not their own—seeking something we might call completion, or perhaps the word clarity will do as well, a goal to which only the spirit's compass points the way.[1]

Pilgrims wander for the love of God. We are persons in motion who have responded to the call of the Spirit to make our journey in often unfamiliar places. We have chosen to make our "home" this life of sojourning with God. Though there is an element of lostness in the concept of "wanderer," it is also true that those who wander as pilgrims are not lost. We have at our disposal many tools to discern the Spirit's compass and find our way. In the following pages I want to remind us of these tools and of the ways they might be deployed as we make our pilgrimage.

MAPS IN OUR ATLAS

Humankind has used maps as a way of charting the landscape of our lives for at least 4,300 years. Whether we are referencing the clay cuneiform maps of Mesopotamia of 2300 BCE or the GPS-connected maps in a car's navigational system, we are familiar with the way maps work. The map is a rendering of the landscape that has a certain correlation to the world. That correlation is never 1:1. It is typically some ratio of space on the map versus distance in the world—miles per inch, for example. We understand that the map is a trustworthy but only suggestive description of the reality of the world through which we navigate. It is not an exact rendering of reality. If a map's ratio to reality was 1:1, then it would no longer be a map—it would be the world in which we live. This is an important concept to keep in mind as we consider the maps that provide guidance to the pilgrim.

Actually, it would be more accurate to say *atlas* than maps. An atlas is a collection of maps, charts, illustrations, diagrams, and so on, which together provide a rich resource for navigation, orienteering, and understanding. Pilgrims have at our disposal something closer to an atlas than a single map. Our atlas is made up of the combined guidance offered by these sources:

- The Bible
- The witness and counsel of faithful people past and present
- Our own life story with God
- Tools like the pilgrim's compass, the Pilgrim's Prayer, and the liturgical calendar

The Bible

For many Christians the Holy Scriptures are the rule of faith and manners. While we join with other streams of the Protestant Reformation in crying *sola scriptura* (by Scripture alone), it is important to keep in mind that even a high estimation of the value and authority of Scripture as the rule of faith and life must also acknowledge that this "map" in our atlas does not have a 1:1 correlation with the world in which we live. It was never intended to be read and understood literally, and to use it literally will cause us to be lost more often than we need to be.

The map of the biblical witness is given a privileged place in the atlas as a guide of unsurpassed value and trustworthiness. Faithful pilgrims will regularly immerse themselves in reading and contemplating God's Word in Scripture and will do well to have the Bible with them throughout life and especially when they travel as pilgrims to distant places. Several techniques for engaging with Scripture can help to guide and govern the pilgrim's way. Immersion in the Psalms has been a foundational use of Scripture since ancient times. The most obvious way to immerse in the Psalms is to engage in daily prayers that use psalms as centerpieces. Classically this was done through praying the daily office,[2] but there are simpler and still very effective means to keep oneself immersed in the Psalms. Calvin urged that we should pray regularly throughout the day, and modern Presbyterians have a very strong resource to aid in this practice, the *Book of Common Worship, Daily Prayer*, which provides all 150 psalms with psalm tones for singing; liturgies for evening, night, morning, and midday prayers; and many other resources.[3] The practice of praying regularly through the Psalms and, over time, discovering that they are somehow a part of you has shaped many Christians for nearly two thousand years. All of the saints of the church ancient and modern seem to have been immersed in the Psalms, and any pilgrim would do well to follow their example.

Another way to let Scripture provide a map is to consider our lives in relationship with a particular biblical narrative or story. For example, after reading the early chapters of the book of Exodus, I might reflect on my own participation in economic systems that are exploitative and never make good on their promises to me. I might wonder if I have it in me to depart Pharaoh's Egypt and set out with God to a new land of promise. As I see how often the Israelites struggle to maintain trust and hope, I might recognize how often I too am double-minded in my commitments to God and God's ways. Viewing my own life through the lens of the exodus narrative is a way of reflecting prayerfully about my own journey as I ponder the witness of Scripture about the journey of the people of God in the time of Moses.

We can also practice a contemplative way of reading scripture, *lectio divina* (sacred reading). This way of praying with Scripture trusts in the power of God to speak to us in contemplative silence and in a prayerful encounter with the Scripture. Whole books have been written on the process and practice of *lectio divina*, and I need not repeat that material here. To get started with this prayerful encounter with Scripture you need only a little initial guidance about the process. A very basic and general *lectio divina* process is outlined in the box below.

The scriptural map is a richly detailed and complex map that can offer guidance and help in orienting and reorienting us as we wander with God. It is a faithful and reliable record of the witness of countless forebears in faith who lived their own journeys of faith and who recorded their testimony about the nature of God and of God's people.

LECTIO DIVINA
A simple four-step engagement with Scripture:

Lectio

(Read)   [*read Scripture passage twice*]
Silence 3–5 minutes*—silently repeat a word or phrase that interests you . . .
Sharing aloud (if in group): Simply share the word or phrase that spoke to you. No elaboration.

Meditatio

(Reflect)   [*read once*]
Silence 3–5 minutes—reflect on "Where does this Scripture touch my life? How does it relate to me?"
Sharing aloud: "I hear, I see, I was struck by . . ."

Oratio

(Respond)   [*read once*]
Silence 3–5 minutes—reflect on "How is God calling me to respond? What needs to be done?"
Sharing aloud: Briefly pray, spontaneously expressing your response to God's call.

Contemplatio   **(Rest)**   [*read once*]
Rest in the Word, in silence 2–3 minutes. Rest in God's grace.

The time allotted for each period of silence can vary.

The Faithful Witness of Fellow Pilgrims

To the witness of Scripture we add the witness of faithful people past and present who have proven by their words and deeds to be exemplary followers of Jesus. In the third chapter of Philippians, the apostle Paul writes, "Brothers and sisters, join in imitating me, and observe those who live according to the example you have in us" (Phil. 3:17). The practice of watching and imitating the lives of faithful disciples is a biblical way of growing in our discipleship. Some of these witnesses will be of ancient origin (the saints of the church), and other will be our contemporaries. Still others we will know only through their literary witness in books, blogs, poems, and so forth. God has always provided the community of faith women and men who provide trustworthy examples of what it looks like to live as a child of God and a follower of Jesus. We can learn much from these pilgrims who have traveled the path before us and who can provide much-needed guidance, correction, and encouragement.

The Reformed tradition, with its strong focus on Scripture as the rule of faith and life, has perhaps been guilty of neglecting the maps provided by the lives and writings of people of faith down through the ages. Fortunately, there has been significant effort in recent decades even among Protestant traditions to reclaim the voices of the faithful from our common past. While we do not give these the same reverence and authority that are rightly reserved for Scripture, the lives of the saints, the writings of early Christians, and the poetry and prose of the mystics can all be of great value in helping us to find our way as we seek to follow Christ.

In particular I find the *Sayings of the Desert Fathers*[4] to be a rich trove of spiritual guidance that, though it comes from a distant location in both time and geography, nevertheless seems to be a prescient source of correction and guidance to the twenty-first century. Classics like Augustine's *Confessions* and the poetry of John of the Cross can also be very provocative. More recent authors and saints of the faith who have given us great help include Thomas Merton, Henri Nouwen, Carlo Carretto, Teresa of Calcutta, and Evelyn Underhill, to name only a few. The pilgrim might take up the writings of one of these literary mentors and read for a year or more in order to be totally immersed in their wisdom and guidance.

It is also likely that each of us knows someone who shines as an example of faithful wrestling with the demands of faith and who seems to be a joyful and Spirit-led disciple of Jesus. Maybe it is someone in our family, or a friend at church, or a colleague at work. We can learn much from observing these contemporary saints. In my own life, one of these saints was my mother, who was alive in her faith and who demonstrated for me what it looks like to find and maintain a living relationship with God. Another contemporary saint was my seminary professor, friend, and mentor Ben Campbell Johnson, who repeatedly proved to be a reliable guide. Ben's deep wisdom, his profound humility about what he could know with certainty, and his abiding hope and trust in the power of God to make his life meaningful all serve as an inspiration for me.

It is part of God's wisdom and grace that we are given saints of the faith—both ancient and modern—who can be reliable guides as we make our own journey. These saints are "maps" of a sort who can assist us as we attempt to remain oriented with God ever before our eyes.

Our Own Life Story

Our atlas includes the story of our own life. By reflecting on our life history and on the ways we can see God's presence in it, we can decipher clues about the present journey in which we find ourselves. Spending time in prayerful and attentive reflection on our spiritual autobiography can provide a great deal of guidance for our pilgrimage of faith.

Pilgrims are sometimes surprised at the suggestion that their own life is a "map" to be used in the ongoing journey of faith. Perhaps they think, "But I haven't been a particularly devout disciple." The story of our life can be instructive both in the times when we got it right and followed the calling of the Spirit of God faithfully *and* as a record of the times when we went down what was clearly a "dead end" path. A review of our life with God that seeks to illuminate both our successes and our failures can be helpful. We learn to be gentle with ourselves about the times we strayed, understanding that our straying can also be instructive, and we learn not to be too proud of our victories, recognizing that even our successes are derived from God's prevenient grace.

The practice of examen, which comes to us from the Ignatian tradition, is an important discipline for reviewing our daily discipleship and can also be modified to help us in making a life review. The next section provides a modified examen process organized around the points of the pilgrim's compass.

The Compass

The compass rose, which is found on nearly all maps, has many variations in complexity; most commonly it indicates the four cardinal directions (north, south, east, west). The eight-point compass rose (or wind rose, as it is sometimes named) includes the intercardinal directions (northwest, northeast, etc.). These map compass roses were used from ancient times (long before the invention of a reliable magnetic compass) to aid in the orientation of maps. Most maps were oriented by reference to celestial bodies—the sun being the most frequent and obvious choice. Each day's journey began with orienting the map to the sun at its rising. It is not surprising that for Europeans, Asia was described as the Orient, because it is in the east, the direction that oriented one's map. After the introduction of a reliable magnetic compass in the twelfth century, it became common to orient maps with reference to magnetic north. What is important to us as pilgrims is this discipline of orienting the map. The map, as powerful a tool as it is, is made many times more powerful when it is correctly oriented, and if it is not properly oriented the map can actually lead us away from our intended destination.

If we think of the Bible, and the lives of saints past and present, and our own life story as "maps" for the journey, then it is critically important that they are properly oriented. So, for example, many Christians stop to pray a prayer of illumination prior to engaging in reading, studying, or preaching from Scripture. The prayer is meant to acknowledge that apart from God's help in showing us what we need to see and opening our ears and minds and hearts to God's Word, we will do little that is helpful. We "orient" ourselves and our engagement with Scripture by intentionally returning our attention to God and seeking God's help in discerning what the "map" of Scripture is saying to us. Similar prayers might correlate with our devotional reading of the life of a saint, or our reflection on our own life.

A compass has several powerful aspects that can be useful to us as we journey with God. As mentioned above, it was common in ancient times to daily orient one's map by seeking out the place of the sun at its rising. You can also recalibrate and make corrections to your orientation at day's end by noting the place of the sun's setting. An old idea might help us here. A third-century bishop of Carthage, Cyprian, wrote the following about evening prayer:

> Also at the sunsetting and at the decline of day, of necessity we must pray again. For since Christ is the true sun and the true day, as the worldly sun and worldly day depart, when we pray and ask that light may return to us again, we pray for the advent of Christ, which shall give us the grace of everlasting light.[5]

Note the curious phrase "Christ is the true sun and the true day." Cyprian is speaking poetically here, but perhaps we can follow him in orienting the map of our daily walk with God by turning and returning our attention to Christ.

The most basic and biblical pattern for this kind of prayerful attention is that we return to God in prayer when we lie down and when we rise up.[6] This allows us to reconnect our day to God and to reflect on how we might live it more faithfully. This pattern follows a typically Hebrew way of counting the day, by beginning not at sunrise but at sunset. Remember, for example, how the days are described in the Genesis account of creation, "There was evening and there was morning, the first day" (Gen. 1:5). Patterns of daily prayer have traditionally followed this evening start of the day. That may seem odd to us who often think of our days beginning with sunrise, but it has a long history in the practice of daily prayer.

The decision to begin our day in the evening rather than the morning has subtle but important theological import. When we arise with our day planners in hand and begin our days with morning, it is easy to be driven by our own agenda. When we start our day at evening and soon go to sleep, we shift our understanding. God now works for about eight hours while we sleep, and when we arise we prayerfully ask, "What have you been doing, Lord, and how can I join you in that now?" Rather than setting our own agenda, we are conscious of beginning our day in the middle of God's day and joining with God in God's work.

Traditionally, the prayers at the hour of sunrise, called Lauds, are organized around the desire to praise God for the gift of a new day in which we can enjoy God's gifts and live obediently in God's grace. At the hour of sunrise we ask, "What are you doing today, God, and how can I join you in your work?" We pray at Lauds, "O Lord, open my lips, and my mouth will declare your praise" (Ps. 51:15). And we profess, "The steadfast love of the LORD never ceases, his mercies never come to an end; they are new every morning; great is your faithfulness" (Lam. 3:22–23).

At sunset we return to God in prayer in a service commonly called Vespers. At Vespers we give thanks for our day and practice the daily examen by which we hope to identify those places where we are succeeding in our discipleship and also those places where we need further growth. Below is a version of the examen that can be used individually or with a group at day's end. It connects to the pilgrim's compass, which will be more fully explored in the following pages.

DAILY EXAMEN

Thanksgiving

I give thanks for this day in every circumstance—understanding that both joys and sorrow, victories and defeats, illness and health are opportunities for me to grow in self-understanding and in my knowledge of God. Today I was most grateful for the following . . .

Encounter

Lord, you have promised, "When you search for me, you will find me, if you seek me with all your heart." As I reflect on this day, where have I sought you and where have I encountered you?

Struggle

Lord, I struggle to keep the faith and to live ever more fully into true discipleship. Today I struggled to respond to your loving invitation by . . .

Wounding, Wandering, Weakness

Lord, I pray to gain the wisdom of the apostle Paul, who wrote, "Therefore I am content with weaknesses, insults, hardships, persecutions, and calamities for the sake of Christ; for whenever I am weak, then I am strong." In what ways, today, have I experienced wounding, wandering, or weakness?

New Name

Lord, you are always calling us into the sorts of adventures that turn Abram and Sarai into Abraham and Sarah; Jacob into Israel; Saul into Paul; Simon into Peter. Today how will I allow you to lead me into a deeper discipleship which promises new life?

Finally, the word "compass" in Latin derives from words for "step together." For pilgrims this too can be an instructive thing to notice. Our pilgrimage is not typically made alone. We are on the way with other pilgrims who can help us find the way and make the journey safely. One of the most beautiful gifts pilgrimage offers is the opportunity to "step together" with other friends in faith as we are "journeying together with friends on the path to a Spirit-led and joyful life."[7]

A Pilgrim's Prayer

A few years ago I composed a prayer for pilgrims. This has become an important prayer used by those pilgrims who have been on the journey with me in recent years. A number of pilgrims have memorized the prayer and use it daily as a way of reminding themselves of the journey they have undertaken. Others have used it on travel pilgrimages to keep them attentive to the sacred nature of their travel. This prayer, and a host of other prayers for pilgrims, can serve as a resource in our atlas to provide a brief and memorable distillation of the hopes of pilgrimage. Notice the repeated petition, "Lead me, Lord," which is found only in Psalms. There is no more central and unifying petition in the heart and mind of a pilgrim than that the journey be led by the calling of God.

A Pilgrim's Prayer

Lead me, Lord,
gently, pervasively, irresistibly, increasingly,
so that I walk my pilgrim way steadily,
and find the place of my resurrection.

Lead me, Lord,
so that I neither dally nor disobey,
nor turn aside, nor stand still, nor stumble,
nor turn back in loyalty to old gods
who will not bless me.

Lead me, Lord,
as a felt Presence,
as a constant companion,
as a counselor in perplexity,
as my first, fast, last friend.[8]

Lead me, Lord,
by the restlessness of spiritual longing,
by the hope of finding my true home,
by the yearning of a hungry heart.

Lead me, Lord,
by grace to gratitude,
by gratitude to generosity of spirit,
by generosity to mercy,
that I may cultivate a compassionate heart.

Lead me, Lord,
through your loving embrace,
so that I do not forget or fall away,
but remain steadfast and loyal,
joyful and true on my journey with you. Amen.

The Liturgical Calendar

An important resource in the pilgrim's atlas is the liturgical calendar. The liturgical year shapes our experience of time and hallows time too, when we are attentive to it. The liturgical calendar is, itself, a repeating itinerary of God's pilgrimage among us and our sojourn with God. Beginning with Advent we recall that God made a pilgrimage to us in the life of Jesus, and that God will come again in the final consummation of God's redemptive work. Arriving as it does in proximity with the winter solstice, the movement from Advent through Epiphany is a movement from darkness to light. Baptism of the Lord reminds us of our own baptism. Transfiguration of the Lord reminds us of the hope that we will come to see things as they really are. The long arc that bends from Ash Wednesday, through Holy Week and Easter, and beyond to Pentecost is a movement from ashes to newly kindled flame. Within that long arc we practice penitential self-examination, enter fully into the horrors of Good Friday, and rise up in joy at the marvel of resurrection. The long stretch of Ordinary Time, which defines the summer months and into the fall, is a reminder that much of our faith is lived out in the ordinary activities of life. We conclude with the confident declaration that Christ is King.

Volumes have been written to tease out the depths of the mystery of time made holy by attention to the liturgical calendar. It is enough here to simply acknowledge that any pilgrims who are attentive to the narrative that the calendar supports will begin to see their own journey as a reflection of the story of God's journey. That is no small thing, for when we begin to perceive the mystery of our own life as it connects with the life of God given through the Holy Spirit, we begin to discern deeper and deeper truths about ourselves, about our neighbors, and about God too.

The Pilgrim's Compass

In the early 2000s, I was introduced to the pilgrim's compass by a friend. As we spoke about travel, he mentioned that he had just returned from a pilgrimage to the Holy Land, where he had met Dr. Henry Ralph Carse, who was in Jerusalem working with the Kids4Peace organization.[9] Dr. Carse had shown him the compass, which my friend then drew for me. The pilgrim's compass is captured in the logo for the Pilgrimage.[10]

Like the compass roses of maps of old, the pilgrim's compass invites us to orient ourselves. Only this time we orient our life in reference to God and ask where we are in our journey with God. The pilgrim's compass is meant to be used daily as a way of inviting prayerful reflection on the content of our life before God. It is used when we are at home traveling the path of pilgrimage that is ordinary discipleship and it is used when we are on a travel pilgrimage, to aid in the daily reflection on our holy journey.

The compass has *E* at the top and then, in clockwise order, *S*, *W*, and *N*. We will go into far greater detail about this in the final chapters of this book, but for now let us note that these correspond with common aspects of our journey with God:

E = Encounter
S = Struggle
W = Wounding, Wandering, Weakness, or maybe Wilderness
N = New Name, Newness

We make sense of our wandering lifestyle as follow-ers of Jesus by not wandering aimlessly. Pilgrims wander-ing with God are not lost. But let us not underestimate how easy it is to stray. We are prone to wander in self-directed paths where we can easily lose sight of the God we love. So we make use of the tools we need to wander with purpose:

- The inner compass of the Spirit's calling
- The maps that make up our atlas
- The community of fellow pilgrims
- The pilgrim's compass

Using these tools, pilgrims can create a community through which we learn to hear the call of God and respond in faith, "journeying together with friends on the path to a Spirit-led and joyful life."

QUESTIONS FOR REFLECTION AND DISCUSSION

1. Who are the saints in your life—people who are trust-worthy examples of faithful discipleship? Do you have literary mentors whose writings are guides for your faith?

2. Psalm 26:3 says, "For your steadfast love is before my eyes, and I walk in faithfulness to you." The daily disci-pline of orienting our life toward God is a way of keeping the steadfast love of God ever before us as we sojourn faithfully in God's truth. How will you practice daily ori-entation to God? Morning and evening prayer? Practic-ing the examen based on the pilgrim's compass?

3. "Lead me, Lord!" This phrase starts every section of the Pilgrim's Prayer. How is the Lord leading you? In

what ways do you cooperate with or resist the Lord's leading?

JOURNALING AND PRAYER EXERCISES

1. Choose one or more of the following biblical narratives and journal about the ways the narrative can be understood in relationship to the points on the pilgrim's compass: Encounter, Struggle, Wounding/Wilderness, New Name:

   • Jacob in Genesis 32
   • Abram and Sarai in Genesis 12–17
   • Peter in Matthew 16

2. Practice a walking prayer. Go for a daily walk and begin with the simple prayer "God, show me what you want me to see." Then make your walk, maintaining attention to the things and people you encounter. Be on the lookout for what God desires to show you.

3. Reflect on your own spiritual journey and begin to think of your journey in terms of the pilgrim's compass. Choose one time to write about, identifying your encounter with God, your struggle, the wound/wilderness, and the new name with which you limped away.

SUGGESTED BOOKS FOR FURTHER READING

Ben Campbell Johnson and Paul H. Lang, *Time Away: A Guide for Personal Retreat* (Nashville: Upper Room Books, 2010).

Richard Morgan, *Remembering Your Story: Creating Your Own Spiritual Autobiography* (Nashville: Upper Room Books, 2002).

Office of Theology and Worship for the Presbyterian Church (U.S.A.), *Book of Common Worship, Daily Prayer* (Louisville, KY: Westminster John Knox Press, 2018).

Beau Riffenburgh, *Mapping the World: The Story of Cartography* (London: Andre Deutsch, 2015).

Margaret Silf, *Compass Points: Meeting God Every Day at Every Turn* (Chicago: Loyola Press, 2009).

Chapter 4

THE PILGRIM'S COMPASS—
ENCOUNTER

The first point of the pilgrim's compass is *E* or "encounter."
When we daily orient our life toward God we can expect
to grow in our awareness of the daily encounters we have
with our Lord. Thomas Merton writes of the extraordinary
place of encounter with the glory of God, noting both its
elusiveness (it comes only as a gift) and its ubiquity (the gate
of heaven is everywhere):

> At the center of our being is a point of nothingness
> which is untouched by sin and by illusion, a point of
> pure truth, a point or spark which belongs entirely
> to God, which is never at our disposal, from which
> God disposes of our lives, which is inaccessible to
> the fantasies of our own mind or the brutalities of
> our own will. This little point of nothingness and of
> absolute poverty is the pure glory of God in us. It is
> so to speak His name written in us, as our poverty, as
> our indigence, as our dependence, as our son-ship.
> It is like a pure diamond, blazing with the invisible
> light of heaven. It is in everybody, and if we could
> see it we would see these billions of points of light
> coming together in the face and blaze of a sun that
> would make all the darkness and cruelty of life vanish

completely. . . . I have no program for this seeing. It
is only given. But the gate of heaven is everywhere.[1]

How do we encounter God? And is that something we
control? Or are our encounters gifts freely given by God
but never under our control? Merton writes that he has
"no program for this seeing," no formula to teach us that
will reliably give us the vision of which he writes so powerfully. "But," Merton insists, "the gate of heaven is everywhere." The Christian tradition has long contemplated the
pathways to our perception of these gateways to encounter with God. Surely Brother Lawrence is on to something
when he teaches us to practice the discipline of being truly
present to each moment with an expectation of encounter.[2]
Jean-Pierre de Caussade too urges us to be attentive to our
encounters with God in each present moment.[3] While it
seems clear that we cannot conjure encounters with God
through any technique that we control, there is much that
we can do to heighten our sensitivity to the presence of God
in each passing moment.

　　We meet God in this world—not eating pie in the sky
when we die. I grew up in Greenville, South Carolina, and
though my own church did not speak this way, the overall
Christian culture of the deep South in the 1960s and 1970s
often focused on an expectation of meeting God at some
future event (death, the Rapture). I was well into my seminary training before it really began to sink in to me that my
relationship with God was not principally about securing
my mansion in heaven for some future circumstance, but
rather, my relationship with God was much like my relationship with those closest to me—*an ongoing and daily
encounter with the person of God* who by grace chose to
befriend me.

As an undergraduate music major I performed Mendelssohn's *Elijah* and memorized the words, "If with all your heart Ye truly seek me, Ye shall ever surely find me. Thus sayeth our God!"[4] The pilgrim's compass has *E* at the top, and the *E* reminds us that we have encounters with God. And further, these encounters are not limited to some future situation, but are common to all of us daily. One of the most important spiritual disciplines therefore is to cultivate the awareness of our encounters with God.

Our encounters with God are more frequent when we are attuned to the world of the Spirit. When Jesus promises us that the Spirit will come to us, in chapter 14 and following in the Gospel according to John, he is alerting us to be mindful of the world of the Spirit. That world in which the Spirit is present surrounds us like air, it impinges on our thoughts, it is full of gentle invitations, and it awaits our attention.

Our encounter with God sometimes requires that we go looking for it. I am reminded of an old rabbinical story I heard years ago. As the story goes, a rabbi was keeping watch over his grandsons. The two boys were playing hide-and-seek, and the older boy hid first. The younger child searched and searched until he found his brother. They then changed roles, with the younger child hiding. The rabbi later was approached by the little one, who was crying. He said, "Tevi, what's the matter?" The little boy answered, "We were playing hide-and-seek and I hid and Saul didn't even look for me!" The old man took the child in his arms and comforted him. A bit later Tevi noticed that his grandfather was crying too. He said, "Pappa, why are you crying?" The old rabbi replied, "It is the same with God. God is hiding and no one is even looking for him." God is sometimes experienced by us as a master of hide-and-seek.

We must go in search of the one we love and who is hidden everywhere if we can just adjust our eyes to see, our ears to hear, and our hearts to embrace our loving Lord hidden in the ordinary experience of each moment.

We meet God both in turmoil and in peace. We might be tempted to isolate our sense of encounter with God to those mountaintop moments of joy or wonder or those quiet moments when the world is hushed and still. God, no doubt, can be encountered in those moments. It is also true that encounters take place in the midst of turmoil and trouble. Scripture gives many examples of people who cry out and who find that God is listening and eager to help. Think of the Hebrew slaves in Egypt in Exodus 2. Think of the harrowing escape at the shore of the Red Sea in Exodus 14. Think of Psalm 107 with its case studies of God's faithful rescues. Think of Jesus in his postresurrection appearances bringing "peace" to his disciples in the fearful days following the crucifixion.

When I was in my midthirties I went through a difficult season of clinical depression. It took many years for me to recover. I spent many days in prayer during that time, hoping desperately for some kind of rescue, some kind of relief. One day as I sat in the empty sanctuary at Monastery of the Holy Spirit in Conyers, Georgia, I knew that God was with me in that place. And more than that, I knew that God loved the pathetic wretch I considered myself to be. I sat and prayed and wept, because for the first time in my life I was experiencing amazing grace—a love that was not waiting for me to get my act together, or for me to recover, or for anything. I knew that God loved me as I sat there, and I mark that moment as the true beginning of my recovery from deep depression. If God could love me even knowing who I was, then maybe I could learn to love myself again—even knowing who I was. My encounter came in the midst of the turmoil of a painful depression.

Sometimes our encounter with God is like a burning bush. Though sometimes when I am trying to sort out a difficult decision I wish that God would be more directly present, I also agree with C. S. Lewis, who observed that sometimes in our prayers we have an encounter with God that delivers more than we bargained for.[5] I had one of those "more than I bargained for" moments in prayer as a child. Growing up in a devout community, I learned as a young child that I should ask God to come into my heart. I am sure that I learned this at the Baptist vacation Bible school I attended with a friend. So one night when I was about seven years old (with my dog Peggy curled up at my feet) I rather mechanically went through the prayer asking God to come into my heart . . . and something happened! I was stunned and a little scared. It was hard to describe later, but it was the first time I knew that when I prayed there was *a person* on the other end of that prayer who was listening and who just might act in a way I could sense. It was exciting, and a little unnerving, and now I never belittle the experience of those Christians who have encountered God in a direct way because, while it has rarely been so flashy in my experience, I too have had a burning bush of sorts.

More often most of us encounter God as a still, small voice. A biblical narrative beautifully describes this:

> "Go out and stand on the mountain before the LORD, for the LORD is about to pass by." Now there was a great wind, so strong that it was splitting mountains and breaking rocks in pieces before the LORD, but the LORD was not in the wind; and after the wind an earthquake, but the LORD was not in the earthquake;

and after the earthquake a fire, but the LORD was not in the fire; and after the fire a sound of sheer silence. When Elijah heard it, he wrapped his face in his mantle and went out and stood at the entrance of the cave. Then there came a voice to him that said, "What are you doing here, Elijah?" (1 Kgs. 19:11–13)

I love the way Brother Carlo Carretto writes of this.

> God's call is mysterious; it comes in the darkness of faith. It is so fine, so subtle, that it is only with the deepest silence within us that we can hear it. And yet nothing is so decisive and overpowering for a [person] on this earth, nothing surer or stronger. This call is uninterrupted: God is always calling us! But there are distinctive moments in this call of his, moments which leave a permanent mark on us—moments which we never forget.[6]

Most of the time I think many of us experience our encounters with God and the call to pilgrimage in this subtle way. We yearn for something, and we start searching out what it might be. We spend weeks or even years in prayer slowly sorting out what it is we think we are hearing and only then come to a confidence about what we are asked to do. It is less an "aha!" moment and more like an incrementally growing clarity that what we desire is consistent with what we think God desires for us.

The encounter with God happens in the encounter with strangers. This is one of those peculiar things one notices when reading Scripture. God is often discovered in the encounter with strangers. We find this with Abraham and Sarah at the oaks of Mamre, with Jacob at the river

Jabbok, with Jesus' disciples on the road to Emmaus and on the shores of the Sea of Galilee, and many other places too.[7] This has important implications for pilgrims. We answer the call to pilgrimage recognizing that part of our journey is to put us in the places where encounters with strangers are almost impossible to avoid. Our task is to keep in the forefront of our mind that each and every encounter is a potential encounter with the risen and present Lord.

An additional aspect of "stranger" must not be overlooked. Particularly when we travel on pilgrimage, we are choosing to become a stranger among other strangers. We set out on a journey that is certain to take us to places where we are not ensconced among familiar habits, familiar foods, and familiar people. Being the stranger can be a pathway to more fully understanding our Lord who came to dwell among strangers and to practice a gracious and redemptive way of life. As we look for and expect to find Christ in the others around us, we also consider how we are meant to be an expression of God's love in the way we travel.

There is also a way in which we can be a stranger and grow through interaction with strangers even when we are not traveling, or at least not traveling far. We can grow in this way by engaging in work near our home aimed at creating a workable human community. Often this will bring us to encounter the strangers who are close to home. For me this happened through the ministry of Habitat for Humanity. I got involved in building affordable housing in my hometown when I was in my twenties and was astonished to realize how insulated my life had been. Though I had grown up there and lived there for more than twenty years, I was unaware of the experiences that some of my fellow Greenvillians were having in terms of substandard housing. Habitat for Humanity helped make strangers into friends as I worked alongside a wide variety of my neighbors in creating simple, decent housing for all. Similar experiences happen at food pantries, clothes closets, and a host of other ministry settings.

Recently, as I was teaching about our encounters with God, I invited the students to share times when they encountered God. At first everyone chuckled when one student said, "I encounter God when I come home and my dog joyfully greets me." However, as the seconds ticked by, I could see a better understanding sink in as people recalled their own encounters with a pet whose love was full of grace. The capacity of your dog to love you in spite of your many foibles is legend. It is why we have T-shirts with the "prayer," "Today I am trying to be the person my dog thinks I am." Many of us have been shaped by a religious culture focused so effectively on our guilt and need for shame that we have lost touch with the reality of grace—an unmerited and unexpected inclusion in someone else's love. When my student named her encounter with God as something she experienced in the encounter with the delighted reception from her dog, she was naming that experience of grace.

Sometimes a place becomes a place of encounter. Many pilgrimage destinations are places where people over many years have felt an encounter with God occurring. The site becomes a place of pilgrimage because it seems to be a place where the veil between the ordinary and the holy is very thin. After a time, the place becomes immersed in the prayers of millions of people of faith who have visited and prayed over thousands of years, and those prayers too have a way of sanctifying the place.

On a recent pilgrimage to the Holy Land, I found myself with a free day in Jerusalem. I walked to the Church of Saint Anne, a small church with a long history. It is dedicated to Anne the mother of Mary, mother of Jesus. The ancient story is that the church is built over a grotto where Mary is said to have been born. The historicity of this claim is uncertain. However, I sat in St. Anne's for hours on my free day in Jerusalem. I prayed, I journaled, and I watched as countless pilgrims came and went. St. Anne's marks the beginning of the Via Dolorosa, so nearly every pilgrim to Jerusalem finds their way to St. Anne's, if only for a brief glimpse inside before beginning the walk of the way of sorrow. As I sat quietly amid the churn of hundreds of pilgrims coming and going, I was keenly aware of the many prayers that had been offered to God in that space since its creation in the early twelfth century. By the time I left hours later, the historicity of the claim about the church being over the place where Mary was born had become totally incidental to me. What was undeniably real, faithful, beautiful, and true was that the place was made holy by the faithful people who came and offered something of themselves to God in that sanctuary—as I myself had done.

We encounter God through the Word of God in Scripture. We can be reading a portion of the Bible and come to realize that it is not just a story about someone else, but in some mysterious way is a word meant for us. My encounter with Psalm 127 was such a moment. It happened at a time when I was very ambitious and hard working. I was spending an unhealthy number of hours trying to accomplish good ministry through sheer grit and determination. I was also feeling the symptoms of burnout and fatigue. My friend and mentor Ben Johnson suggested that I spend regular time in the Psalms, and after only a few weeks of casually reading the Psalms I came across Psalm 127 and immediately realized that it held an important word for me, personally. The psalmist writes near the beginning, "Why do you rise up early and go late to your rest, eating the bread of anxious toil? Do you not know that God loves you and desires to gives you rest?" (au. trans.). I knew as soon as I read the words of the psalm that I had encountered a word of God which held an important corrective for me. The psalm was no longer *just* a psalm. It had become a word of God for me personally.

The heavens are telling the glory of God. Certain landscapes seem to open us up to an encounter with God. Traditionally these are mountains and desert landscapes. I know that whenever I am walking in mountainous places with vast vistas around me, I do feel a sense of joy and wonder at God's creativity. I also feel a sense of peace, awe, and wonder when on the prairies of the Midwest or the moors of Northern Scotland—anywhere that there is a big sky created by unobstructed views to a distant horizon. There is a way in which God speaks to us through the landscape, and once we begin paying attention to the impact that the surrounding landscape has on our spirit, we are often better able to hear God trying to say something to us. Indigenous people and their various faith traditions have often been far more attentive to this aspect of encountering God. Christians too can find encouragement to seek encounters with God in the wonders of the world in, for example, the creation psalms (Pss. 8, 19, 104, and 148, to name only a few).

Practices lead to encounter. As the previous pages suggest, the pathways to our encounters with God are as varied and unique as our individual lives, but we can learn from one another and from those who have come before how to live before God with a deeper attention and expectation of encounter. Those who desire to perceive these encounters and who are willing to be disciplined in their spiritual formation will be blessed. Practical ways to do this include:

- **Open your eyes.** Ask God to show you what you need to see, and then pay attention.
- **Listen with your ears,** particularly to the voices of those who are often silenced.
- **Be reflective about your life.** Keep a journal, practice the daily examen, wonder.
- **Be fearless in the face of change.** Ask, "What can God show me now that would have been hard for me to know before the change?"
- **Pray.** It is the lifeblood of your relationship with God. Any of a thousand ways to pray will do.
- **Cultivate compassion.** Because God is so often encountered in another person, it is a great help to you to learn to be faithful and merciful to those around you.
- **Pay attention to your inner yearnings.** What makes your heart sing? God is probably in that!
- **Serve.** Remember that both the sheep and the goats in Jesus' parable (Matt. 25:31–46) were surprised to realize that they were encountering God in their interactions with "the least of these."
- **Learn from the saints.** Let the witness of Scripture and the counsel of the great saints of the church be your companions along the way.
- **Find and feed a Christian friendship** with someone who can help you discern the ways in which God is being encountered in your life. Spiritual direction is also a good way to do this.
- **Worship regularly.** There is no substitute for the practice of worship. Daily worship is not too often.

Our encounters with God are often an invitation to change or to follow and thus to enter a liminal[8] state where there are foreshadowings of something new coming to life within us. For this reason our encounters often include a measure of resistance and struggle within us. The nature of the struggle that our encounter with God provokes is the subject of the following chapter, on the second point of the pilgrim's compass. It is enough here to simply notice how often this encounter-struggle pairing occurs in Scripture. Jacob encounters God in the stranger at the river Jabbok and immediately wrestles (struggles) with God through the night. Saul is knocked from his feet and forced to deal with his blindness on the way to becoming the great apostle who writes many of the epistles included in the New Testament. The disciples who encounter Jesus struggle to understand, struggle to be faithful as followers, and struggle to keep courage in the time of trial. Having examined our encounters with God, let us now consider the struggles that are often paired with encounters.

QUESTIONS FOR REFLECTION AND DISCUSSION

1. Think about a time when you encountered something holy. What was that holy moment like? Was it connected to a place or an experience you had? How did the encounter with the Holy change you?
2. How do you think that times of change and transition open us up to encounters with God?
3. What landscapes evoke wonder and awe in you? Have you experienced an encounter with God that was connected with a particular landscape?

JOURNALING AND PRAYER EXERCISES

1. In prayer, present yourself before God. Pay attention to the present moment and be alert to the holiness of the presence of God with you in the present moment. Let your mindfulness of God continue after the time in prayer ends and you return to your daily activities so that all of your life remains infused with the sense of the holiness of each present moment.

2. Our encounters with God are often an invitation to change or to follow and in so doing to enter into a liminal state where there are foreshadowings of something new coming to life within us. Where are you encountering God at this time in your life? Have you considered how God may be inviting you to something new? How does the encounter evoke either resistance and fear or hopeful anticipation in you?

SUGGESTED BOOKS FOR FURTHER READING

Carlo Carretto, *Letters from the Desert* (Maryknoll, NY: Orbis Books, 2002).

Tilden Edwards, *Living in the Presence* (New York: HarperCollins, 1994).

Belden C. Lane, *The Solace of Fierce Landscapes: Exploring Desert and Mountain Spirituality* (New York: Oxford University Press, 1998).

Brother Lawrence, *The Practice of the Presence of God* (New Kensington, PA: Whitaker House, 1982).

Chapter 5

THE PILGRIM'S COMPASS—
STRUGGLE

Often our encounters with God lead to struggles. Resistance to change, fear of leaving what is known, doubts about God's reliability to provide what is needed—all these (and other struggles too) are common responses to the moment of encounter. This chapter explores the nature of these struggles and suggests that our relationship with God is struggle worthy, and that the struggles can be instrumental in our discovering who we truly are.

In the twelfth chapter of Luke's Gospel, Jesus says, "Do you think that I have come to bring peace to the earth? No, I tell you, but rather division!" He has just finished telling the parable about servants who were given talents, and concludes that "from everyone to whom much has been given, much will be required; and from the one to whom much has been entrusted, even more will be demanded." Our encounters with God often demand a decision, a new commitment, and a determination to turn from one path and begin walking another. Jesus repeatedly warns that we cannot serve two masters, that we must choose whom we will serve, and in so warning us he echoes the word of the Lord given through Moses. This requirement that we choose definitively whom we will love and serve often creates a struggle, because whether we name it "concupiscence," as Augustine of Hippo did, or "idolatry," as John

Calvin did, we can all recognize the many things we love and serve that are inconsistent with the heart of God. Like our biblical ancestors, we are often double-minded and easily stray from our loyalty to God alone. It is good to consider this struggle to which the *S* of the pilgrim's compass points.

The relationship is worthy of struggle. To say that part of our struggle is with the *relationship* is to acknowledge that we are not called to follow an idea, but rather a person. In fact, God in three persons. It is significant that the early church defined the Trinity in terms of the "persons" of the godhead: God who is parent, God who is sibling, and God who is advocate. Each of these points to our relationship with a living God. All significant relationships are complex and require an investment of time and a commitment to persevere in times of trouble.

And there is more. The relationship is a relationship of love as opposed to indifference. God is not far-off and disinterested in us. God is close by and even "in" us in some mystical way. This God who is so near often listens to our cries and also offers us a word in reply. God's Word typically startles and pushes us to reconsider our settled assumptions, and thus it is a means to both endless grace and endless disputation. Like any authentically loving relationship, our relationship with God provides room and safety for real engagement with the kind of give-and-take that defines abiding love. God, out of love for us, occasionally breaks God's own rules and reconsiders God's own plans in light of our input. In this way, love introduces struggles both within us and within God because God allows God's love of us to introduce a real impact on God as a result of the relationship.

This relationship is worthy of the struggle. It is valuable enough, meaningful enough, and impactful enough to be worth the struggle. We struggle because we know that this relationship is capable of providing rich blessings. Sometimes like Jacob at the river Jabbok, we have to wring a blessing from this relationship by wrestling earnestly (see Gen. 32).

When we struggle we are in good company. Think of the many times in Scripture when people encounter God and then struggle to respond in faith. I have followed Scripture itself in often naming Abram as an example of someone who heard the call to "go" and responded. It is true that Abram's initial response seems like a paragon of faithfulness; in Genesis 12:4–5, he hears the call and leaves with Sarai, his wife. However, at the very first moment of testing (just seven verses later Genesis 12:11–13) Abram proposes that Sarah lie and tell the Egyptians that she is his sister. She is then taken into the king's consort! Thankfully the Egyptian king sorts it out and sends both Abram and Sarai on their way.

When Moses encounters God in the burning bush and learns of his call to return to Egypt, he struggles with that call. He asks, "Who am I that I should go to Pharaoh, and bring the Israelites out of Egypt?" (Exod. 3:11). And later as Moses wanders the deserts with the people of God we see another moment of encounter and struggle. Moses by this point has had enough of his newfound calling as leader of Israel. The people are all complaining and Moses goes to God to say, "Did *I* give birth to these people? Did *I* suckle them to my breast? The burden of this people is too heavy for me, and in fact, if you love me—kill me" (au. paraphrase of Num. 11:10–15).

Peter and the other disciples who have encountered God in the risen Christ nevertheless return to their old work as fishermen until Jesus comes again to remind them that they are fishers of people now (see John 21).

When our encounters with God lead us to struggle, this is a common response, and we can take solace in the knowledge that some of God's favorites (Abraham, Moses, Peter) all struggled in the wake of their encounters.

We struggle to understand. If you are like me, you have a baseline assumption that most things can be understood, and that when we understand them, we can master them. This way of thinking is part of Enlightenment reasoning, and it is an often unexamined assumption at the heart of much of our thinking about the nature of things. The idea is that if you come to know something and can break it down into its most basic units, and then reassemble it, you then truly understand it.

An easy example of this line of thinking is Newton's experiments with light. Newton began to study light and found (with the use of the prism) an astonishing discovery—white light is not "simple." It is complex, made up of the colors found in a rainbow. Prior to Newton everyone assumed that white light was simple. Newton also discovered that he could not further break down the light into even more colors (when you put indigo light through a prism you do not get additional colors), so he knew that the colors the prism gave him were the most basic ones. He then discovered that a second prism, properly positioned, could reconstitute the rainbow into white light again. By Enlightenment standards, he understood (and had mastered) white light by demonstrating that he could break it into its most basic parts and reconstruct it. But we have good reason to ask if he really understood light. Indeed, light continues to elude our efforts to fully understand it.

Our relationship with God and with God's thoughts is similar. "'My thoughts are not your thoughts, nor are your ways my ways,' says the LORD" (Isa. 55:8). We sometimes struggle with this relationship with God because it defies our efforts to master God through understanding. While we can come to know God and to know God's will, we have to hold such knowledge gently—understanding that it is always a partial knowledge and always in some respects flawed. Reformed Christians have this humility about their knowledge when we admit that our understandings of God are reformed and always reforming.

It is also important for those of us who place great value in understanding to realize that understanding is not always the solution.

> When . . . Abba Anthony thought about the depth of the judgements of God, he asked, "Lord, how is it that some die when they are young, while others drag on to extreme old age? Why are there those who are poor and those who are rich? Why do wicked men prosper and why are the just in need?" He heard a voice answering him, "Anthony, keep attention on yourself; these things are according to the judgement of God, and it is not to your advantage to know anything about them."[1]

We struggle to let God be God. If Genesis 3 has it right, then one of the most persistent habits of the human creatures made in God's image is the desire to be the arbiters of good and evil. In assuming this responsibility we exceed our place and attempt to supplant God, who alone ultimately decides what is good and what is evil.

We also see in the book of Jeremiah another way we struggle to live within the limits of our creaturely nature. Jeremiah powerfully portrays our desire to be self-sufficient and autonomous actors when he declares on God's behalf:

Be appalled, O heavens, at this,
be shocked, be utterly desolate,
        says the LORD,
for my people have committed two evils:
  they have forsaken me,
the fountain of living water,
  and dug out cisterns for themselves,
cracked cisterns
  that can hold no water.

            (Jer. 2:12–13)

We struggle with the pain and trouble of loss. Sometimes our struggle is caused by our assumption that if we are faithful, we will be spared pain and trouble and loss. But even a cursory reading of the Bible should be sufficient to dissuade us from that line of logic. Indeed, the great women and men of faith whose lives are recorded in the Bible are typically in trouble and pain precisely because they are faithful.

One biblical example of this aspect of struggle is found in the story of Elijah in 1 Kings 18 and 19. Elijah is faithful to his calling and puts himself at considerable risk to expose the idolatry of the prophets of Baal. Yet rather than being rewarded for his faithfulness, he incurs the wrath of Jezebel and soon is fleeing for his life. He becomes exceedingly discouraged and wishes for death. Thankfully he is met in the wilderness by an angel who urges him to eat and drink in order to be strong for the journey ahead.

More will be said about this when we speak of wounding in the following compass point, but here it is enough to acknowledge that we struggle with the discomfort inherent in every life and wonder what we are to make of our pain and loss in the light of our relationship with the God who loves us.

We have struggles internal to ourselves. When my mother made a pilgrimage to Iona some years ago, she was invited by the pilgrimage leader to think about what she wanted to leave behind. This is an old practice for those going on pilgrimage. People will abstain from alcohol consumption, or stop smoking, or vow not to purchase anything unnecessary while on pilgrimage. Pilgrims identify some aspect of life that impedes their life with God, and they leave it at home as they set out on a travel pilgrimage. My mother knew exactly what she desired to leave behind— it was that little (but persistent) voice in her head that her whole life had been telling her that she was not enough. It was the voice of criticism and judgment that left her perpetually feeling unworthy and inadequate. Before she passed away, she gave me her journal from that pilgrimage, and in the journal I can see her engaging with that voice. She writes, "I see you, little voice of criticism. You do not belong with me here. Now fly away home. I am on pilgrimage!" Sometimes our struggles are internal, and they vary from person to person, but we can use the struggles to help us grow in our reliance upon God.

Years ago I was in the midst of a long and self-deprecating prayer in which I was offering to God my laundry list of faults and foibles. Somewhere along the way I became distracted by a daydream. In the daydream my son Daniel (who was four years old at the time) was kidnapped. In the home we owned at the time we had a rule that Daniel was not to play in the front yard. There was a busy street in front of the house, so we told him to play in the fenced backyard. In my daydream, Daniel was playing in the front yard and someone in a car pulled up, grabbed him, and drove off. In my daydream Sarah and I were beside ourselves with grief and worry. Several days passed, and then as Sarah and I stood in the front room of the home, the car pulled up and Daniel hopped out and ran up the sidewalk. I burst out of the front door and down the stairs, racing to sweep him up in my hug. As he ran to me he was crying and saying, "Daddy, I'm sorry. I'm sorry. I know I wasn't supposed to be playing in the front yard." As I hugged him I thought to myself, "I don't care anything about that. I'm just glad you are home!" Instantly I was returned to my prayer and I realized that God is not much interested in my endless confessions. God is only glad that I have come home again. I now make confession succinctly and try to be honest but not to dwell inordinately upon my faults, preferring instead to be swept up in God's loving embrace.

We struggle with a world that is not always radiant with the love of Christ. Sometimes our encounter with God authorizes a departure from previously held assumptions about how the world works and to whom we owe a debt of love. We find ourselves advocating for those unable to defend themselves and exhorting people and systems to show a generosity to the marginalized whom the system is not pleased to serve. Sometimes we struggle not with God but with a world that refuses to participate with God in the creation of a workable human community. This aspect of our struggle is complex because on the one hand we struggle against those systems and powers that oppose the vision of God. On the other hand, our struggle may be to acknowledge the ways in which we, ourselves, have too easily adopted the habits and values of a darkened world.

Struggle can be asceticism. Our struggle does not always need to be interpreted as a sign of infidelity or as a sign that we are somehow failing to engage properly in faith formation. Sometimes the struggle is what it looks like to do what must be done. The word "ascetic" in ancient times described athletes in training. Understood in this way, what we are doing when we adopt an intentional asceticism is to let go of some things in order to focus on other things. For example, athletes have to stop eating junk food and watching TV all day in order to make time to perfect the many skills needed to excel in their sport. They must train in a disciplined way in order to develop stamina to run their race to the end. A similar process happens with musicians who make time to perfect the playing of their instrument through rigorous and disciplined rehearsal.

It is not so different when we consider our spiritual life. If we desire to grow significantly in our relationship with God, we must be willing to let go of behaviors that keep us from God and to embrace the disciplines that will help us grow. Though our commitment to growth will sometimes require us to struggle, pilgrims gladly engage in disciplines that foster a deepened relationship with God and bring vitality and joy to the journey.

Travel pilgrimage as a discipline also adds its own struggles. The difficulties inherent with travel are many:

1. When traveling alone on pilgrimage, the potential for isolation is real. There is a reason that so often people travel on pilgrimage in company. The companionship of fellow pilgrims provides safety in numbers as well as a trusted set of companions with whom you can sort out the meaning of your journey. But traveling companions bring complications too.

2. When traveling in a company of pilgrims, you must learn the grace-filled art of submitting your own personal preferences to the will and needs of the larger company of pilgrims. This happens over things as insignificant

as determining a location for the next meal and things as important as making substantial changes to the itinerary. I recall a day in a pilgrimage not many years ago when I was nearly undone by a woman in the bus seat behind me. She had a persistent and sickly sounding cough, and for an hour as I rode along in front of her I felt everything but compassion for someone who was ill. I felt trapped at not seeing another seat I could move to. I felt fear that she would make me sick. I felt anger that she would board an enclosed mode of transport knowing that she was coughing her germs for all of the rest of us to breathe in. None of those thoughts are Christlike and I am proud of none of them, but they are a good example of how the discipline of traveling presents its own struggles. I have traveled on pilgrimage now with many groups and have both watched this struggle in others and experienced it in myself. Belonging to a company of pilgrims will test your capacity for patience and grace.

3. Your planned itinerary is seldom completed as you envisioned because of the inevitable variability of weather, mood, and circumstances beyond your control. In 2008 when I was on pilgrimage to Europe, I was stranded unexpectedly with my wife and children in a little town in Italy several hundred kilometers from our destination. Because we did not speak Italian, and because the train station was a remote one without much foot traffic, it took over an hour for me to learn that a nationwide transportation strike was under way and there was neither rail transit nor bus nor taxi to get us to Florence. There was nothing to do but sit in an empty train station for twelve hours, trying to keep my sons entertained. It was nearly 3:00 a.m. when we finally walked the last two miles into the heart of Florence to awaken our B&B host and finally fall exhausted into bed.

In 2015 we were on pilgrimage to Iona when a great

storm engulfed the region, and for days no ferries were allowed to come to the island. We began to fear that we would be trapped on Iona indefinitely when, unexpectedly, there was a lull in the winds and a few ferries ran their routes. We *just* got back to the mainland in time to continue our travels. Learning to adjust to the changing circumstances of travel pilgrimage is an essential discipline for pilgrimage. And more than just acceptance of the circumstance, there is a spiritual aspect of learning to ask, "What is this new and unexpected situation trying to teach me? Where is God in this?"

As the previous pages make clear, there are a great number of ways that we can struggle as pilgrims. Our struggles hold important clues to answering the question, "What is God wanting from me now?" Having honed our ability to perceive our encounters with God and having considered how those encounters often lead to struggle, it is now time to think about the *W* of the pilgrim's compass—a compass point that signals wounding, weakness, and bewilderment.

QUESTIONS FOR REFLECTION AND DISCUSSION

1. This chapter has offered comment on a number of ways pilgrims often struggle: to understand; to let God be God; to cope with the pain of loss; to overcome internal doubts and self-criticism; and so on. Which of these struggles resonates with you? Or are there other struggles you might name?

2. The Bible is rich with stories of the people of God struggling to understand and to remain faithful to their covenant with God. In what ways are those biblical stories similar to *our* stories?

3. Abba Anthony struggled because he could not understand why things happened the way they did. When he asked God about it, he was told that sometimes things happen for reasons he could not know, and that even if he *did* know, the knowledge would not help him. Do you think that is true? Why do you think that we are so desirous to know the "why" of this life?

JOURNALING AND PRAYER EXERCISES

1. Take some time to name and acknowledge your current struggle and offer it in prayer, taking time to listen for God's loving response leading you as you embrace God's peace at this time in your life.

2. The use of the pilgrim's compass is a discipline of daily considering where we are in our journey with God and taking time to reconnect with God in an effort to remain oriented toward the goal of following Jesus. Use the pilgrim's compass for a week or more as the tool for your daily reflection about your discipleship.

SUGGESTED BOOKS FOR FURTHER READING

Walter Brueggemann, William Placher, and Brian Blount, *Struggling with Scripture* (Louisville, KY: Westminster John Knox Press, 2002).

Joan Chittister, *In God's Holy Light: Wisdom from the Desert Monastics* (Cincinnati: Franciscan Media, 2015).

Francois Fénelon, *Let Go* (New Kensington, PA: Whitaker House, 1973).

Chapter 6

THE PILGRIM'S COMPASS— WOUNDING, WILDERNESS, WANDERING

The pilgrim's compass as it was first described to me follows the narrative arc of Genesis 32: Jacob encounters God in a stranger, wrestles or struggles with him at the river Jabbok, is wounded in the struggle, but limps away clutching the blessing of a new name. Thus you get in one concise narrative a tidy movement through the compass points encounter, struggle, wounding, and new name. As I have lived with the compass over the years I still resonate with wounding, but I also can think of other words to which this point on the compass seems to apply and which begin with a *w*. Wilderness, wandering, and weakness are all appropriate options for the *w*. But before we leave the rich possibilities of a word like "wounding," let us pause and reflect on how that might be just the right word.

WOUNDING

Very few of us are content with our wounds. Our wounds come in a wide variety of forms. Sometimes they are physical; at other times they are psychological. There are spiritual wounds, too, caused by encounters with bad theology or unhealthy communities of faith. The discomfort that our wounds bring and the weakness to which they seem to point are not easily reconciled with the world's way of defining success. The world celebrates what is strong, influential, spectacular, and beautiful. Of course, the zealous pursuit of these things encourages denial of the reality of any weaknesses or wounds. The church, when it is at its best, provides a place where disciples are safe to make an honest appraisal both of their strengths and gifts, and of their weaknesses and wounds. As Jesus taught in John's Gospel, we are meant to know the truth and to let that knowledge set us free (see John 8:32).

It is tempting to believe that our trust in God will ensure that we are never wounded—that our faith somehow insulates us from the slings and arrows of a fallen world. And yet, even a cursory reading of the Gospels discloses to us that Jesus himself suffered much in the course of his life: Born to peasants who were soon fleeing as refugees to a foreign land, he lived as an itinerant teacher with no apparent source of income beyond the gifts of strangers, suffered much at the hands of the religious leaders and political authorities of his day, and died in ignominy. It becomes clear that when God sojourned among us as one who was fully human, he too had to cope with wounds.

Wounds are sometimes a part of the process of redemption and healing. We find this idea throughout Scripture:

> For you, O God, have tested us;
> you have refined us as silver is refined.
> *(Ps. 66:10, au. trans.)*

The process of purification of silver requires that the dross be burned away, leaving what is precious in a purer form. Malachi 3:3 describes a similar work of God.

We remember when Moses offered us words of warning:

> When you have eaten your fill and have built fine houses and live in them, and when your herds and flocks have multiplied, and your silver and gold is multiplied, and all that you have is multiplied, then do not exalt yourself, forgetting the LORD your God, who brought you out of the land of Egypt, out of the house of slavery, who led you through the great and terrible wilderness, an arid wasteland with poisonous snakes and scorpions. He made water flow for you from flint rock, and fed you in the wilderness with manna that your ancestors did not know, to humble you and to test you, and in the end to do you good. (Deut. 8:12–16)

In the teaching of Moses, God brings about redemption by bringing people out of impossible circumstances *but* accomplishes that by leading them through terrible wildernesses and wastelands, full of trouble and danger. The arduous path from enslavement to freedom will humble us and test us and, in the end, do us good. Contrast the teaching of Moses with the typical and popular prosperity gospel you can hear on any Christian radio station or Christian television channel, which teaches that following God leads you to prosperity, and you can see why so many of us struggle to embrace our wounds.

In the Gospel according to John, when Jesus makes his postresurrection appearances he is often among the disciples in some miraculous way—he appears in a room when the door is locked, for example. And yet, though his appearances are clearly miraculous, the disciples are not convinced by his spectacular appearance among them. It is only after he shows them his wounds that they rejoice because they know he is the risen Lord. *Christ is known to them by his wounds.* There is a lesson in this for those of us who are followers of Christ. We so often want to be recognized as his ambassadors and as his servants, but we want to engage in ministry to others from a position of strength. This can be seen when our ministries of compassion are one-sided, when there are those who serve and those who are identified as needy. But, in truth, we are all needy and we all have gifts to give.

Benedictine monasteries in ancient times would reply to a knock on the door with the question, "What gift do you bring?" The question stemmed not from greed or from a requirement that those coming in search of help pay for it. Rather the question grew out of the conviction that all who presented themselves at the door of the monastery were to be treated as Christ. The underlying assumption was that God was sending the person to the monastery with a gift that they could uniquely provide. It was a way of honoring the one knocking by trusting that they had a gift to give, and it was a way of flattening out the hierarchy of need by showing that the monastery needed things too. Perhaps we would be more authentically our Lord's disciples if we were willing to let our wounds and our neediness show more often.

Every spring for the last fifteen years I have met with a group of twenty friends in Atlanta. For many of us this means making a pilgrimage of sorts because we live far away from Atlanta. We gather, we pray the daily offices, and we meet in small groups to share our lives. Each year, we begin by providing each person a chance to share what has been happening in the year since we last met. As the group has grown in trust, these "check-in" statements have become more and more transparent on the subject of wounds. People simply tell it like it is, and the rest of us are glad for the courage of the speaker to name wounds among the celebrations and to trust that God is at work in both the joys and the sorrows. The capacity of this group to speak authentically about not only places of strength and success, but perhaps even more importantly about places where we are wounded, has led to a resilient community of faith.

We are at liberty to pray to God about our wounds. We would be in good company if we were to ask that God remove them from us (the apostle Paul comes to mind). However, we might hear in reply something similar to Moses' speech from Deuteronomy 8 quoted above, or something like God's reply to the apostle Paul, which will be described in the section on weakness below.

In recent years as I have made a number of pilgrimages, I have had to come to terms with my own wounded nature. I take my wounds with me on pilgrimage, and my pilgrimage is not improved by my denial of wounds nor by my efforts to ignore them. My pilgrimage is enhanced when I make my wounds simply another place where I can meet God and be made new. The God who loves us and whom we seek after on our pilgrimage is a God who is wounded, and we should not be surprised to discover that if we want to be with God we must be willing to go to places that wound. Our discipleship is made more authentic and real when we stop pretending everything is OK and begin to wrestle with our wounds. When our wrestling takes place in the context of a company of pilgrims, then we have the potential that both we and they can "bear one another's burdens, and so fulfill the law of Christ" (Gal. 6:2 RSV).

WILDERNESS

There are, of course, many wilderness narratives in Scripture, but I am thinking of the departure from Pharaoh's Egypt as recounted in the book of Exodus. They were escaping with God's help from enslavement to a system in which they were endlessly working for diminishing returns. Pharaoh was never going to treat them justly or pay them fairly for lives spent in service to his pyramid scheme, so when Moses came offering an alternative life with the Holy One of Israel, they gathered their courage and departed the fertile Nile delta and marched out into the wilderness. They were almost immediately sorry and began complaining:

> The whole congregation of the Israelites set out from Elim; and Israel came to the wilderness of Sin, which is between Elim and Sinai, on the fifteenth day of the second month after they had departed from the land of Egypt. The whole congregation of the Israelites complained against Moses and Aaron in the wilderness. The Israelites said to them, "If only we had died by the hand of the LORD in the land of Egypt, when we sat by the fleshpots and ate our fill of bread; for you have brought us out into this wilderness to kill this whole assembly with hunger." (Exod. 16:1–3)

I chuckle every time I read these verses. They are saved from Pharaoh and his chariots in chapter 14, and most of chapter 15 is dedicated to singing God's praises for the powerful and wondrous rescue they had just experienced. Then exactly two verses into chapter 16 they start complaining! How quickly we people of God forget, and how quickly is our distrust of the new life exposed.

We do remember what life was like in Pharaoh's economy, where all the benefits trickled to the top of the pyramid and all the toil and harsh treatment belonged to us. We learned in Egypt that Pharaoh (who claimed to simply want more bricks) actually just wanted to abuse us. We have lived under the tyranny and hopelessness of brick making for far too long. We know that the life offered in that rat race is not the "good life." It is a form of half-life, a shadow of the real thing. So we yearn with all of our hearts to escape enslavement in a life that is not really life at all . . . and at the same time, we so easily look back in nostalgia and desire to return to it. Our duplicity is confusing until you remember that Egypt is not without its enticements.

Years ago, after a session of spiritual direction with one of the brothers at Mepkin Abbey in which I rambled on and on about my complicated life, my spiritual director, who had said almost nothing for an hour, got up to leave, then turned back to me and said, "Your affluence will not make you happy—but it might just keep you comfortable in your unhappiness." With that he gently left me alone with God to wonder about my affluence, my unhappiness, and the many ways I claimed to want one life (that of a faithful disciple) and yet remained committed to another (just another rat, running like the devil in the rat race).

If pilgrimage is analogous to walking with God out into the "wilderness" of choosing to disengage from the economics enslaving us (and I think it is), then it is no wonder that we find the wilderness so disorienting. When we are so fully enmeshed in a world of accumulation where there are no free lunches and where all benefits must be earned, choosing to follow God into a wilderness in which manna falls through no effort of our own seems like silliness. I think we find the need to rely on God for our daily bread deeply disorienting. Grace is bewildering to those who are committed to a meritocracy in which we all get what we earn. How ironic that we pray frequently without noticing the radical departure our words are trying to signal: "Give us this day our daily bread."

Perhaps I am too focused on the economic aspects of wilderness . . . but if we consider that "economics" derives from the Greek *oiko*, "house," and *nomos*, "rules" or "laws," it is not hard to see how these ways of thinking about ourselves and our life with God are infused in all aspects of our discipleship. Manna falling in the wilderness is analogous to grace abounding for the sinner. The bewildering experience of having all our former ways of defining ourselves (and others) flattened out by the common experience of everyone gathering manna each morning and having the same amount whether we gathered much or gathered little is analogous to the apostle Paul's assertion, "There is no longer Jew or Greek, there is no longer slave or free, there is no longer male and female; for all of you are one in Christ Jesus" (Gal. 3:28).

Pilgrimage as a discipline of faith formation is an intentional decision to depart from Egypt and the life that is killing us and embark upon a wild odyssey of self-discovery in which we not only rediscover our relationship with the God who leads us and who provides the manna and water, but also rediscover our neighbors and know them to be just like us in every significant way.

And there is more. When we engage in the discipline of pilgrimage, we are choosing to spend our money and our time not on the accumulation of greater wealth and possessions, but rather on the treasure of a deeper and more resilient relationship both with God and with our neighbors. Our relationship with God is enriched as we learn to trust that when we risk a wilderness sojourn with God, God will provide. The manna will fall. The water will flow. As Moses asserts in Deuteronomy 8, not even the clothes on our backs will wear out. Our relationship with our neighbors is strengthened because living in the wilderness requires neighborliness. We cannot successfully traverse the wilds on our own. The only way to arrive at the new promised land is for the community of God's people to join hands and start marching—*together*.

When my son was small, I was leaving a grocery store in Greenville, North Carolina, with too many plastic bags clutched in both hands. My poor son was trapped under my right arm and was slipping out, so that I nearly had him in a headlock as I walked across an asphalt parking lot so hot you could see the waves of heat rising in the air. A kindly woman, noticing my plight, walked over and offered to help. I said, "No, thanks. I think I've got it!" As I put my bags in the car a few minutes later and drove home, I found myself wondering, "What is wrong with me that I am so resistant to admitting my need for help that I would choke my son all the way across a parking lot before accepting assistance from a kindly neighbor?" Now, looking back on that moment, I think I can finally answer the question. I was unable to acknowledge my need for help because I was still living in a worldview that taught me that I was responsible for myself. I did not want to admit my need for help nor be entangled in a sense of obligation to my neighbor, so I refused the help I obviously needed. The wilderness can be a place that teaches us better than that and restores in us the calling to help God in the creation of a workable human community.

Finally, the role of wilderness in asserting our principal identity is seen in Jesus' own baptism, where he is told,

"You are my beloved," and then immediately he departs for a season of wilderness wandering during which he is enticed with other ways of defining himself. He is tempted to be the one who makes bread from stones, who spectacularly survives a fall from great heights, and who is defined by great power. It is during his post-baptismal wandering that he confirms that his truest self is the Son of the Father.

We too, of course, are tempted to define our value by a myriad of attributes—wealth, power, beauty, influence, intellect—and pilgrimage invites us to leave those behind while we wander in the wilderness with God, in the hope of returning us to an unalterable conviction that whatever other merits we may possess, what matters most is that we are God's beloved children.

WANDERING

The *W* of the pilgrim's compass is suggestive not only of wounds and wilderness, but of wandering too. As I mentioned in a previous chapter, I am a bit of a homebody. It makes my attraction to the discipline of pilgrimage that much more ironic. I tend to plan my travel carefully and am not much naturally inclined to wander. However, several times in my life I have said to God, "I will go anywhere you send me." Each time I got in reply some version of Genesis 12:1–4: "Go from your father's house and your kindred and your country to the land that I will show you . . . and I will bless you so that you can be a blessing by which the world is blessed" (au. paraphrase). And each time I was blessed by my willingness to wander for the love of God. My first call in ministry was to Arkansas, and it blessed me richly. More recently, in 2012 I accepted a call to Fargo,

North Dakota, and my years of sojourning in North Dakota have been filled with blessings. Though I am inclined to avoid wandering, I must admit that there are gifts that God desires to give me which seem to appear only when I open myself to going wherever the Spirit directs.

When I think of the wandering aspect of pilgrimage, I think of peregrination—the act of wandering, especially to wander as a foreigner. There is a long history of this kind of traveling as a stranger for the love of God. You need only consider the missionary trips of Paul and the other apostles, the many narratives of the Celtic saints who pushed off from shore to wander wherever the tides and winds took them, or more recently the story of someone like brother Carlo Carretto, who left a promising career in the church to traverse the deserts of North Africa in search of God.

Because the discipline of pilgrimage often aims to bring us to a liminal state, it is essential that we regularly cross the threshold of our home life and pass into the broader world where we can become disentangled from the many ways that we typically define ourselves and are set free to consider seeing ourselves simply as God's beloved children again.

WEAKNESS

Though the Bible often speaks of God's power, and the theology of the church has often focused on God's power, it is also true that the God we find in Scripture is a God of weakness too. This is never more convincingly in view than during the events of Jesus' trial and crucifixion. It was a scandal that the early Christian theology was so often preoccupied with the death of Jesus. Everyone knew that the

Messiah wasn't supposed to die and certainly wasn't supposed to die by crucifixion. And yet, the earliest parts of the New Testament were written in service to the message that Jesus died and that his death was somehow connected with God's loving work of redemption for all people. This was as confusing then as it is today. The apostle Paul found himself explaining things to the church at Corinth:

> Where is the one who is wise? Where is the scribe? Where is the debater of this age? Has not God made foolish the wisdom of the world? For since, in the wisdom of God, the world did not know God through wisdom, God decided, through the foolishness of our proclamation, to save those who believe. For Jews demand signs and Greeks desire wisdom, but we proclaim Christ crucified, a stumbling block to Jews and foolishness to Gentiles, but to those who are the called, both Jews and Greeks, Christ the power of God and the wisdom of God. For God's foolishness is wiser than human wisdom, and God's weakness is stronger than human strength. (1 Cor. 1:20–25)

The apostle Paul also recounts his own struggle to understand how his wounds and the weakness they bring could be a part of his redemption in his second letter to the church at Corinth:

> On behalf of such a one I will boast, but on my own behalf I will not boast, except of my weaknesses. . . . To keep me from being too elated, a thorn was given me in the flesh, a messenger of Satan to torment me, to keep me from being too elated. Three times I appealed to the Lord about this, that it would leave

> me, but he said to me, "My grace is sufficient for you,
> for power is made perfect in weakness." So, I will
> boast all the more gladly of my weaknesses, so that
> the power of Christ may dwell in me. Therefore I am
> content with weaknesses, insults, hardships, persecu-
> tions, and calamities for the sake of Christ; for when-
> ever I am weak, then I am strong. (2 Cor. 12:5, 7–10)

Thus we see the early theology of the Christian community wrestling with the truth of power clothed in weakness.
Indeed, power "made perfect" in weakness. Paul writes
eloquently about how the resurrection points to this weakness that is, in truth, power. The body sown in the grave
becomes the spirit raised in imperishable form; the person
buried in weakness is raised in power. These divine ironies,
first understood in relation to Jesus and his death and resurrection, become mysteries applied to all who follow him.
Just as we have shared his image in the flesh, so we will bear
his image in heaven (see 1 Cor. 15:42–49).

There is another benefit to claiming and being at
peace with our weakness. It can lead us to have a proper
dependency on God. When we are proud and powerful,
we can imagine that we are self-made and self-sufficient.
Accepting the limitations of our weakness inclines us to
turn to God for help in times of trouble. If this is true for
individuals, it is also true for church congregations. Too
often the church has assumed power and growth to be the
measures of health and vitality. The logic has been that
faithful congregations will, by definition, be growing and
powerful congregations. Therefore, weak and shrinking
congregations live with the nagging suspicion that they
must have done something wrong. Perhaps they have. But
perhaps, just maybe, they are being invited in their weak-

ness to trust that God is with them still and that the time of weakness is a time to renew their faith—to learn again to hope for things not yet seen.

Of all the points on the pilgrim's compass, I find the *W* point the hardest to embrace. I naturally retreat from encounters with my own wounds or weakness, and the pilgrim's compass is a daily reminder to me that my wounds, my weakness, my seasons of wilderness wandering—these are all a natural part not only of life in general, but of my faith journey in particular. The pilgrim's compass invites me to befriend the wilderness and to embrace my wounds as places where I can meet God and be more authentically the person God calls me to be. In the next chapter we will examine that blessing which sometimes comes to us in the midst of our encounters, struggles, wounds, and wandering—a new name.

QUESTIONS FOR REFLECTION AND DISCUSSION

1. "Perhaps we would be more authentically our Lord's disciples if we were willing to let our wounds and our neediness show more often." Reflect on that statement with others and share not only your thoughts, but also how you feel when you honestly do this.
2. "Grace is bewildering to those who are committed to a meritocracy in which we all get what we earn. How ironic that we pray frequently without noticing the radical departure our words are trying to signal: 'Give us this day our daily bread.'" Reflect on these familiar words of the Lord's Prayer in light of our willingness or resistance to meet God in the wilderness and trust for God's guidance, provision, and protection.

3. This chapter quotes Moses from Deuteronomy 8, cautioning us to remember that God brought us out of slavery through hardships and these, in the end, were meant to humble us and do us good. While not all wounding comes from God, Scripture does describe some wounding as part of the redemptive process. Reflect on how this can be true. What resistance do you feel to this? Can you think of something you experienced as a wound that can be seen with hindsight as a part of a new blessing?

JOURNALING AND PRAYER EXERCISES

1. Weave a time of wounding/wilderness/wandering/weakness into your spiritual narrative and reframe or write it from the place of an authentic disciple of Christ, by identifying yourself as a wounded follower of Jesus.
2. "My pilgrimage is enhanced when I make my wounds simply another place where I can meet God and be made new." Journal about this statement and see how God wants to meet you in your current wound and help bring healing and someone or something new from it.
3. In the person of Jesus we can see that faithfulness to God is no insurance policy against the experience of wounding. Indeed, sometimes we are wounded as a result of being obedient to God in a world that does not love and obey God. Journal about the impulse to connect faithfulness with safety and reflect on Jesus teaching the disciples to pray with a prayer that includes the petition, "Save us from the time of trial, and deliver us from evil."

SUGGESTED BOOKS FOR FURTHER READING

Belden Lane, *Backpacking with the Saints: Wilderness Hiking as a Spiritual Practice* (New York: Oxford University Press, 2015).

Henri Nouwen, *The Wounded Healer* (New York: Doubleday, 1979).

Joyce Rupp, *Walking in a Relaxed Manner: Life Lessons from the Camino* (Maryknoll, NY: Orbis Books, 2014).

Chapter 7
THE PILGRIM'S COMPASS— NEW NAME

In Shakespeare's drama *Romeo and Juliet*,[1] Juliet wrestles with the power of names to divide, yet she also observes that a name does not contain the essence of the thing or person it labels. That Romeo is a Montague does present a problem for their relationship, but his surname is *just* a name. A rose, she says, would by any other name still smell as sweet. Our names, as powerful as they are at shaping our identity, are not fixed and are not able to contain the fullness of the person to whom they point. Even so, our names are an important aspect of our identity.

This truth about the power of a name is captured in the stories we tell too. Knowing the name of one's adversary is a key piece of information in foiling their nefarious plans. If, for example, we could only decipher the name of Rumpelstiltskin we could stop fruitlessly trying to spin hay into gold and be free to live happily ever after. During my bout with clinical depression and the years of recovery, I more than once observed that being able to name my troubles was a significant step in dealing with them in a healthy way. With my therapist's help, I took much time and great trouble to carefully delineate the trouble, to name it, and to wonder what to do with it. There is great power in names.

Sometimes we come to realize that our encounters and struggles and woundings or wanderings have so dramatically altered our understanding of our self that it is as if we are a new creation. We are fundamentally changed, and we may even begin to think of ourselves as someone who is newly born. We were "someone," we risked becoming "no one" in the crucible of struggle and wandering with God, and now we see that we have become "someone new." To say it differently, we risked becoming a stranger—a stranger even to ourselves—and in the process discovered that someone new was being born. Both in the Bible and in the liturgy of the church we see the importance of bestowing and knowing our name.

Consider the practice of bestowing a Christian name at the time of baptism or of taking vows in a religious community. We are called by name as the waters of baptism claim us and we are reminded that God's promises are profoundly and personally for *us*. God, too, is named in that sacramental moment. The liturgy for baptism says, "In the name of the Father, and of the Son, and of the Holy Spirit." We are claimed in the name of God. The Christian name points to one's trust that there is, and is meant to be, a connection and continuity between one's natural life and the life of God within—between earthly discipleship and eternal life. There is a long practice of choosing the name of a venerable saint of the church when selecting one's Christian name at moments of transition such as baptism or taking vows in a religious order. To do so is to connect one's own journey and discipleship with the example of faithfulness seen and preserved in the memory of the saint.

The Bible provides a number of stories in which the bestowing of a new name is an important part of the work of God to redeem. Abram and Sarai, who are barren and whom the apostle Paul describes as so old they are "as good as dead" (Rom. 4:19), are renamed Abraham (ancestor of a multitude) and Sarah in Genesis 17, because God intends to grace them with baby Isaac. Jacob, who has been living into his original name, which suggests that he is a usurper, is given a new name in Genesis 32 after wrestling a blessing from the stranger. He is renamed Israel because he is a man who strives with God and prevails (see Gen. 32:28). Simon is called Peter by Jesus, who adds that upon the rock of Peter the church will be built (see Matt. 16:18). The Saul of the book of Acts who approved of the stoning of Stephen and was "breathing threats and murder against the disciples" (Acts 7:58–8:3; 9:1) becomes the apostle Paul who is responsible for many of the epistles of the New Testament. In each of these narratives, the giving and receiving of a new name marks a significant shift in the identity of the person in question. Paul can no longer be the Saul who breathed murder. Jacob who has been a swindler must now be the namesake of the people of God. The giving of a new name marks both the transition to the new identity and the beginning of a lifelong journey to live fully into the newness the name suggests.

God is described in Scripture as the one who knows us intimately and who calls us by name. We see this in the poetry of the prophet Isaiah: "Do not fear, for I have redeemed you; I have called you by name, you are mine" (Isa. 43:1). In the Gospel according to John, Jesus describes himself as the good shepherd who knows his sheep and who calls them by name before leading them (John 10:3). That God knows us by name points to the intimacy of our relationship with God. This is no distant and disconnected God—it is a God with whom we are in a relationship of a first-name basis. Jesus describes this as a relationship between friends (John 15:14–15). In Isaiah we are told that God cannot forget us because we are inscribed upon God's hands (Isa. 49:16).

Names given at birth and rebirth. Most of us are given a name at the time of our birth. Sometimes the name bestowed upon us points to a cherished relationship our parents have or had with a relative or friend. Sometimes our names point directly to the biblical narrative. My two sons, for example, are named Daniel and Benjamin. And sometimes our names are a reminder of the great themes and virtues of the faith: Grace and Hope, for example. In most cases the names chosen for us at the time of our birth are in some way intentional, and the names given may shape us in subtle ways not even considered when they were given. My great-grandfather Hollingworth, from whom I get my middle name, was a poet twice published, a newspaperman, and a preacher who was responsible for founding a number of churches. It is interesting to note the correspondence of his life with my own.

In truth, many names are given to us. We have the name provided by our parents, the family name or surname, and maybe nicknames that stick. My siblings are older than I am—in the case of my brothers, ten and eleven years older. I remember calling one of my older brothers Big'un and him calling me Little'un. Later, close friends in high school dubbed me Wangly. Still other names are more like titles, but they have the effect of defining us. In my first call as a pastor I was in a small town where it seemed as though everyone simply called me Preacher. Later, after much study I earned an advanced degree and became the Reverend Doctor Paul H. Lang. I still can remember how odd the appellation "doctor" felt to me at first. No one who knows me well calls me Dr. Lang, and about the only place the title is used is on my business card. I am reminded of my childhood whenever someone does call me Dr. Lang. I grew up in a city small enough that people often asked, "Are you Dr.

Lang's son?" When I answered that I was, they invariably would say, "Your dad did my [insert friend or relative]'s nose!" In my mind I guess *he* will always be Dr. Lang, and I am just the preacher. Our names, whether given, chosen, or earned, have a way of defining us, and that can be a good thing, but it can also keep us from becoming someone new. As the biblical stories suggest, sometimes the Spirit of God invites us to live into a new name.

When Jesus and Nicodemus have their conversation in John 3:1–8, Jesus tells Nicodemus that everyone must be born from above and this second birth is a product of the movement of the Spirit. If it seems natural to be named at our birth, why not also consider the impulse to be blessed by new names when we have transformational encounters with God that lead us to feel born again?

In 2016 I was on pilgrimage in the deserts of New Mexico with a small group of pilgrims. We were there to search for Christ in the desert. One day we visited Nambé Pueblo, one of the Tewa Pueblos of the northern Rio Grande region. We visited to learn more about Native American spirituality and to observe the dance that was happening that day. The line of dancers was impressive. Dozens of dancers dressed for the occasion lined up. Drummers kept up the tempo of the dance from their position at the edge of the plaza. Along the line there were also a handful of people who acted like marshals for the dance, helping the younger dancers when they encountered problems and keeping those of us who were there to watch at a distance where we would not impede the dancers. The dancers ranged from quite old to quite young. Some were clearly experts who had danced many times, and others appeared to be less experienced. At the end of each line were children who appeared to be about three years old.

Though they were young, they were meticulously dressed in the ceremonial garments appropriate to the dance and they clearly had also prepared to participate in this worshipful practice. Every one of the pilgrims in my group became fixated on a particular little girl. She was last in the dance line, maybe three years old, and she was beautifully decked out in festival clothing, with an evergreen branch in one hand and a cob of corn in the other. She was absolutely precious.

As the dance progressed, our littlest dancer, who by now was the object of everyone's attention, would dance along with the adults. Occasionally she would become distracted by the drums and drummers who were stationed nearby. Slowly she would drop out of the dance, transfixed by the drumming. A marshal would then gently and lovingly place her back in the line, and she would join the dance again. A few minutes later she would see a butterfly and drop her corn while caught up in the total absorption of watching it. Again, the marshal would pick up her corn and gently return her to the dance, and she would take up the dance again with the others. Moments like these went on for nearly an hour as we watched the dance.

In the evening, as we processed our day, my friend and fellow pilgrim Colleen said, "I was given a new name today." We then listened in rapt attention as Colleen described how watching the little girl became for her a kind of mystical vision in which she could see herself in the person of our little dancer. She too, like the little dancer, was in a long line of people of faith whose faithfulness was being taught to her. She too, like the little dancer, was prone to distraction and sometimes getting the dance wrong. And she too was surrounded by the witness of the other dancers and by those people in her faith tradition who like the marshals gently and lovingly returned her to the line when she had strayed. Colleen said, "Today I was given the new name 'precious little corn dropper.'" It was a powerful revelation not only for Colleen but to all of us of the way we live our faith in a long lineage of people who are teaching us the dance, so to speak, and who are treating us like the precious person we are in God's eyes. A day or so later Colleen found and purchased a small corncob charm to be a reminder to her of her new name.

The pilgrim's compass reminds us to be on the lookout for those moments when we come to realize that we have been blessed with a new perspective, a renewed sense of self, a new name. It may be that the other points of the pilgrim's compass more frequently connect to something that we can identify and that we have the sense of living into a new name less frequently than, for example, we experience an encounter or struggle. Nevertheless, the blessing of receiving a new name is a significant one and not easily forgotten.

The process of hearing our new name and of feeling the liberty to inhabit it is strengthened by the practice of pilgrimage. When we make a pilgrimage and remove ourselves (by distance and time) from the many things that identify us at home, we often come to a liminal moment when we can entertain the possibility of being or becoming someone new. A new and deeper discipleship, a new and more confident trust in God's love, a revitalized sense of being alive are part and parcel of our new name.

Our new name is not just about a blessing bestowed upon us for our benefit. Our new names typically include an invitation to share the blessing God has given. It is telling that the imperative that initiates the stories of the patriarchs and matriarchs of the Old Testament includes a specific mention of names, "I will bless you, and make your name great, so that you will be a blessing" (Gen. 12:2). Translating that into a contemporary thought, we might suggest that God blesses pilgrims, and makes their names great, so that they are a blessing to all those they encounter.

We have looked at the practice of pilgrimage as a discipline for individual faith formation and as a resource to facilitate the broader renewal of the church. We have looked at the biblical patterns of pilgrimage and at the history of the practice in the Christian tradition through the ages. We have taken note of the tools a pilgrim might use to stay oriented toward God—most notably, the pilgrim's compass. Now it is time to reflect on pilgrimage as an anticipation of the life to come. In the final chapter we will explore the concept of the eighth day and how our baptisms, our journey through this life, and our expectations for what is to come can be understood as pilgrimage.

QUESTIONS FOR REFLECTION AND DISCUSSION

1. Reflect on your given name. What connections does your name make for you: connections to family; connections to Scripture; or connections to faith?
2. Have you ever changed your name? Maybe even shifted from first name to middle name at some transitional moment in life? What prompted you to change your name? How did the shift in your name change you?
3. If you could choose a new name, would you? What name would you choose, and why?

JOURNALING AND PRAYER EXERCISES

1. "Why not also consider the impulse to be blessed by new names when we have transformational encounters with God that lead us to feel born again?" As you reflect on this question, what new name do you sense the Spirit of God offering you after a recent encounter, struggle, or wounding?
2. Think of the names for God in Scripture: Lord, God, Most High, Holy One of Israel, Jesus, Holy Spirit, Advocate, and others. How do the many names for God fail to capture the fullness of the reality of God? What might that teach you about God and also about your own names?

SUGGESTED BOOKS FOR FURTHER READING

Walter Brueggemann, *Names for the Messiah: An Advent Study* (Louisville, KY: Westminster John Knox Press, 2016).

Henri Nouwen, *In the Name of Jesus: Reflections on Christian Leadership* (London: Darton, Longman & Todd, 1995).

Chapter 8
PILGRIMAGE AS AN ANTICIPATION OF THE EIGHTH DAY

When early Christian theologians[1] read their Bibles, they noticed something intriguing. In the opening chapters of the Bible the pattern for describing time consists of a seven-day week, continually repeated. They observed that the passing of those days was noted through the recurring vacillation between night and day—there was evening and there was morning, a new day. But when they looked at the concluding chapters of the New Testament— the very end of the Bible—they saw something new. There in the final pages of the Revelation of John, in the description of the new heaven and new earth there was a cessation of the seven-day cycle:

> And there will be no more night; they need no light of lamp or sun, for the Lord God will be their light, and they will reign forever and ever. (Rev. 22:5)

In the world to come it would be endless day! That day became known among Christians as the "eighth day." Immediately they began to incorporate the concept of the eighth day into the architecture of churches and into the furniture of the sacraments. In particular, pulpits were often eight-sided, and even more often baptismal fonts were eight-sided to indicate that when one was baptized one was baptized into the promise of the eighth day. Even now you can find octagonal pulpits and fonts and in some cases octagonal worship spaces.

This concept of the eighth day was an important part of the early Christian church abandoning the practice of worshiping on the Sabbath (Saturday, the seventh day) and choosing instead to worship on the Lord's Day (Sunday, the first *and* "eighth day" of the week). This can be seen in early Christian writings of the Apostolic Fathers, like the *Epistle of Barnabas*, which reads in part:

> Further, He says to them, "Your new moons and your Sabbaths I cannot endure." Ye perceive how He speaks: Your present Sabbaths are not acceptable to Me, but that is which I have made, [namely this,] when, giving rest to all things, I shall make a beginning of the eighth day, that is, a beginning of another world. Wherefore, also, we keep the eighth day with joyfulness, the day also on which Jesus rose again from the dead. And when He had manifested Himself, He ascended into the heavens.[2]

They associated the eighth day with the beginning of another world, the establishment of the new heavens and new earth promised in Revelation. That Jesus rose from the dead and made numerous postresurrection appearances on the Lord's Day (Sunday, the eighth day) only reinforced the conviction that God had already begun this work of redemption. So Christians worshiped on the Lord's Day as a way of pointing to the eighth day, and they built their worship spaces to reflect this new understanding.

You may be wondering about the connection of all this to pilgrimage. The connection is this: when we are baptized we begin a pilgrimage into this new reality that finds its fullest expression in the new heaven, new earth, and new Jerusalem that all inhabit the eighth day. A day not followed by night. It is endless day, a day in which we join the saints in the light in incessant praise of God.

In this way, all Christians are pilgrims who are on the way to our home with God. We are all in transit, as it were, and we live day to day making our way home. We live both in the present with its many demands and in the hopeful and joyful expectation that our present pilgrimage is already a participation in the reality of the new creation that God is establishing.

If we were people who had no idea what the destination was going to be, then we would not need to travel in any particular direction. Those who are aimless have no need for maps and compasses and the companionship of fellow pilgrims. It is precisely because we know that we are destined for a life beyond this current journey that we attend so carefully to the path upon which we travel, because our daily transit is but a daily leg on the larger journey into the reality of the eighth day and all that promises for us.

As we make our way into the twenty-first century, the church and the world are in need of such pilgrims. People at peace with life "on the way." People who have an abiding trust in God who will provide what is needed. The world is hungry for Christians who see themselves not as superior possessors of truth, but rather as humble wayfarers who expect to find their Lord in the person of the strangers they meet. The discipline of pilgrimage and the tool of the pilgrim's compass are essential to the formation of the new church that is arising from what has been before. Pilgrims of this way understand that our journey is made in service to God and to our neighbors as we join God in the redemption of all creation.

We pilgrims live in the hope of a new heaven and earth, and we gladly receive our *encounters* with the risen Lord as evidence that our hope is not in vain. We *struggle* gladly as those who understand that some achievements are worth the struggle needed to accomplish them. We endure our hardships and calamities—those places of *wounding and weakness*—practicing the virtue of fortitude because we understand that "suffering produces endurance, and endurance produces character, and character produces hope, and hope does not disappoint us, because God's love has been poured into our hearts through the Holy Spirit that has been given to us" (Rom. 5:3–5). And we joyfully look for those moments of rebirth when we seem to be given a *new name* that will govern our discipleship for a season, a great name entrusted to us that we might be a blessing to others.

NOTES

CHAPTER 1: PILGRIMAGE AND
THE EMERGING CHURCH

1. Benedicta Ward, *The Sayings of the Desert Fathers: The Alphabetical Collection* (Kalamazoo, MI: Cistercian Publications, 1984), no. 7, p. 142. The same sentiment is repeated in a longer narrative about Abba Poemen, no. 6, pp. 165–66.

2. Abba Euprepius, ibid., no. 5, p. 62.

3. Edwin H. Friedman, quoted by Edward W. Beal and Margaret M. Treadwell in the editors' preface to *A Failure of Nerve: Leadership in the Age of the Quick Fix*, by Edwin H. Friedman, rev. ed. (New York: Church Publishing, 2017), xiii.

4. Victor Turner and Edith Turner, *Image and Pilgrimage in Christian Culture* (New York: Columbia University Press, 1978), xiii.

5. The *Shorter Oxford English Dictionary* defines "peregrination" as "1. A journey through life, especially viewed as a temporary precursor of eternal life in heaven. 2a. pilgrimage. 2b. the action or an act of traveling abroad or from place to place; a course of travel, especially abroad, a journey . . . travel."

6. From the mission statement of the Pilgrimage ministry.

7. I am speaking here of the church after the Edict of Milan in 313 CE, which shifted the attitude of the Roman Empire to one of benevolence toward Christians and which paved the way for the Council of Nicaea in 325 and eventually the incorporation

of Christianity as the official state religion under Theodosius in 380.

8. The regions of ancient Egypt along the northern coast with the Mediterranean Sea and the Nile River floodplain.

9. The way of wandering. To be a passerby or to be one who is passing through.

10. Stanley Hauerwas and William H. Willimon, *Resident Aliens: Life in the Christian Colony* (Nashville: Abingdon Press, 1989); Rod Dreher, *The Benedict Option: A Strategy for Christians in a Post-Christian Nation* (New York: Penguin Random House, 2017).

11. Witness the decades spent arguing and indulging in schismatic behaviors by nearly every mainline Christian tradition over issues as widely divergent as human sexuality, ordination standards, biblical hermeneutics, ordination of women, and ecclesiastical structures.

12. You find these sentiments and others expressed in the Barna Group's research into millennial attitudes about church: https://www.barna.com/category/millennials-generations/.

13. Ward, *Sayings of the Desert Fathers*, no. 7, pp. 142–43.

14. My mother, Rita Lang, wrote this at the beginning of her first spiritual journal, late in the 1990s when she was in her sixties.

15. *Onomasticon* (on the place-names in Scripture). In English translation, *The Onomasticon by Eusebius of Caesarea* (Jerusalem: Carta Jerusalem, 2003).

16. There are a number of English translations of this work; my recommendation is *Egeria: Diary of a Pilgrimage*, trans. and annotated by George E. Gingras, Ancient Christian Writers 38 (New York: Newman Press, 1970).

17. Saint Augustine, *Confessions* 10.4 (New York: Penguin, 1961), 210; Gregory of Nazianzus, *Orations* 8.23, in vol. 7 of *Nicene and Post-Nicene Fathers*, Series 2, ed. Philip Schaff and Rev. Henry Wace (1885; repr., Peabody, MA: Hendrickson, 1994).

18. Martin Luther, *Luther's Works* (Philadelphia: Fortress Press, 1966), 44:86.

19. John Calvin, *Calvin's Complete Commentaries*, Kindle edition, Psalm 50:16.

20. John Calvin, *Institutes of the Christian Religion* 3.7.3, trans. Henry Beveridge (Grand Rapids: Wm. B. Eerdmans Publishing Co., 1989).

21. William Tyndale, *An Answer to Sir Thomas More's Dialogue, the Supper of the Lord After the True Meaning of John VI and 1 Cor XI and WM. Tracy's Testament Expounded* (Cambridge: University Press, 1850), 63.

22. According to the Oficina de Acogida de Peregrinos (Pilgrims' Welcome Office) in Santiago, Spain, the number of recorded pilgrims has dramatically risen in the last thirty years, from 2,491 pilgrims in 1986 to 23,218 in 1996, 100,377 in 2006, and 277,915 in 2016.

CHAPTER 2: PILGRIMAGE AS THE HOME OF OUR SOJOURNING

1. This sentence is from the opening paragraph of *Narrow Road* by seventeenth-century Japanese poet Matsuo Bashō, translated by Cid Corman in *Backroads to Far Towns: Bashō's Travel Journal*, Companions for the Journey 5 (Buffalo, NY: White Pine Press, 2004).

2. מָגוֹר

3. בֵּית מְגוּרָי

4. See Deut. 26:5–9, the first creedal statement, which begins, "A wandering Aramean was my ancestor . . ."

5. See Gen. 47:9. The New Revised Standard Version renders the word "sojourn"; the King James Version prefers the translation "pilgrimage."

6. Benedicta Ward, *The Sayings of the Desert Fathers: The Alphabetical Collection* (Kalamazoo, MI: Cistercian Publications,

1984), no. 3, p. 2. Anthony (251–356 CE) offered this counsel when asked, "What must one do in order to please God?"

7. Peter Berger, Brigitte Berger, and Hansfried Kellner, *Homeless Mind: Modernization and Consciousness* (New York: Vintage Books, 1974).

8. Michael Fishbane, *Sacred Attunement: A Jewish Theology* (Chicago: University of Chicago Press, 2008).

9. T. S. Eliot, "Little Gidding," lines 239–42, from "Four Quartets," in *The Norton Anthology of English Literature*, 4th ed., vol. 2 (New York: W. W. Norton & Co., 1979), 2292.

10. Walter Brueggemann, *The Land: Place as Gift, Promise, and Challenge in Biblical Faith* (Philadelphia: Fortress Press, 1977), 4–5.

11. Ibid., 7.

12. Gregory of Nazianzus, *Orations* 8, in vol. 7 of *Nicene and Post-Nicene Fathers*, Series 2, ed. Philip Schaff and Rev. Henry Wace (1885; repr., Peabody, MA: Hendrickson, 1994).

13. Augustine, *Confessions* 10.4.6, in *A Select Library of the Nicene and Post-Nicene Fathers*, ed. Philip Schaff, vol. 1 (Grand Rapids: Wm. B. Eerdmans Publishing Co., 1991).

14. Belden Lane, *The Solace of Fierce Landscapes: Exploring Desert and Mountain Spirituality* (New York: Oxford University Press, 1998), 4–5.

CHAPTER 3: NOT ALL WHO WANDER ARE LOST: TOOLS FOR THE PILGRIM

1. Richard R. Niebuhr, "Pilgrims and Pioneers," *Parabola* 9, no. 3 (August 1984): 7.

2. Historically, these are seven daily times of prayer beginning at sundown and concluding in midafternoon the following day: Vespers, Compline, Vigil, Lauds, Terce, Sext, None. In recent times this pattern is often simplified by collapsing the

"little hours" of Terce, Sext, and None into one service, prayers at midday.

3. Office of Theology and Worship for the Presbyterian Church (U.S.A.), *Book of Common Worship, Daily Prayer* (Louisville, KY: Westminster John Knox Press, 2018).

4. *Apophthegmata Patrum*. Good English translations are available. I am especially grateful for the Penguin Classics publication translated by Benedicta Ward, *The Sayings of the Desert Fathers: The Alphabetical Collection* (Kalamazoo, MI: Cistercian Publications, 1984). The sayings are often short and acerbic. Joan Chittister has provided important commentary on a selection of the sayings in her book *In God's Holy Light: Wisdom from the Desert Monastics* (Cincinnati: Franciscan Media, 2015).

5. Cyprian, Treatise 4, *On the Lord's Prayer*, par. 35, in *The Ante-Nicene Fathers*, vol. 5, *Hippolytus, Cyprian, Caius, Novatian*, ed. Alexander Roberts and James Donaldson, rev. A. Cleveland Coxe (1886; repr., New York: Charles Scribner's Sons, 1903), 457.

6. In Deut. 6:5–9 the people of God are instructed how to maintain mindfulness of God, and part of that is to speak of God with one another and to their children, "when you lie down and when you rise." From early on the community of faith understood this to authorize prayers at sunset and sunrise.

7. From the mission statement of the Pilgrimage ministry.

8. I have borrowed here the final phrase of a poem by Gerard Manley Hopkins, *The Lantern Out of Doors*.

9. For information about Kids4Peace, see www.K4P.org.

10. The concept of the pilgrim's compass was learned from Dr. Henry Ralph Carse (Jerusalem/Vermont), who learned it in the Holy Land from his pilgrim mentor and teacher, the Rt. Rev. John Bayton (Australia). Dr. Carse wrote his PhD dissertation on the contemporary pilgrimage process, in which the pilgrim's compass plays a key role.

CHAPTER 4: THE PILGRIM'S COMPASS—
ENCOUNTER

1. Thomas Merton, *Conjectures of a Guilty Bystander* (New York: Image Classics, 1966), 155–56.

2. Brother Lawrence, *The Practice of the Presence of God* (New Kensington, PA: Whitaker House, 1982).

3. Jean-Pierre de Caussade, *The Sacrament of the Present Moment* (New York: HarperOne, 1981).

4. It is a curiosity to me that Mendelssohn put these words in the oratorio (and in the mouth of Obadiah), because I believe that they belong to Jeremiah, and not Elijah or Obadiah. Cf. Jer. 29:13.

5. C. S. Lewis, *The Screwtape Letters* (New York: Harper-SanFrancisco, 1996), letter 4.

6. Carlo Carretto, *Letters from the Desert* (Maryknoll, NY: Orbis Books, 2002), xv.

7. Genesis 18 and 32; Luke 24; John 21.

8. The seminal work on the concept of liminality is *The Ritual Process: Structure and Anti-structure* (New York: Aldine De Gruyter, 1995), by anthropologist Victor Turner. "Liminal" derives from the Latin word for "threshold," and thus, to be in liminal space is to cross a threshold into a deeper walk of faith. Liminal space is where conversion and transformation happen. See esp. chap. 3, "Liminality and Communitas."

CHAPTER 5: THE PILGRIM'S COMPASS—
STRUGGLE

1. Benedicta Ward, *The Sayings of the Desert Fathers: The Alphabetical Collection* (Kalamazoo, MI: Cistercian Publications, 1975), no. 2, p. 2.

CHAPTER 7: THE PILGRIM'S COMPASS—
NEW NAME

1. William Shakespeare, *Romeo and Juliet*, act 2, scene 2.

CHAPTER 8: PILGRIMAGE AS AN ANTICIPATION
OF THE EIGHTH DAY

1. I am thinking here of Tertullian (ca. 160–225) who speaks of the "eighth day" in his *On Idolatry* and others like Justine Martyr (ca. 100–165), Origen (ca. 185–254), as well as later theologians like Gregory of Nazianzus (ca. 330–389). For a full exploration of the theology of the eighth day and its development over time, see Samuele Bacchiocchi, *From Sabbath to Sunday: A Historical Investigation of Sunday Observance in Early Christianity* (Rome: The Pontifical Gregorian University Press, 1977), 278–302, or for a much-abbreviated summary of the concept of the eighth day, see Aimé George Martimort, *The Church at Prayer: An Introduction to the Liturgy* vol. 4, *The Liturgy and Time* (Collegeville, MN: The Liturgical Press, 1986), 18–19.

2. *Epistle of Barnabas* 15.8–9, in *The Ante-Nicene Fathers*, vol. 1, *The Apostolic Fathers, Justin Martyr, Irenaeus*, ed. Alexander Roberts and James Donaldson, rev. A. Cleveland Coxe (published 1885), available online at Christian Classics Ethereal Library, https://www.ccel.org/ccel/schaff/anf01.vi.ii.xv.html.

CPSIA information can be obtained
at www.ICGtesting.com
Printed in the USA
FFHW020617070219
50465576-55682FF

9 780664 264697